Social Media Marketing Mastery

Unlock the Latest Strategies for
Unstoppable Growth

Ghazwan Alemara

Copyright © 2024 Ghazwan Alemara. All rights reserved.

No part of this publication may be reproduced, distributed, or transmitted in any form or by any means, including photocopying, recording, or other electronic or mechanical methods, without the prior written permission of the publisher, except in the case of brief quotations embodied in critical reviews and certain other noncommercial uses permitted by copyright law.

For permissions requests or inquiries, please contact the publisher at hello@ghazwanalemara.com

Published by ghazwanalemara.com

Contents

Contents 3
Introduction 1
Chapter 1: The Evolution of Social Media Marketing 4
    The Dawn of Social Media 4
    The Rise of Platforms 8
    The Shift to Engagement 13
    Current Trends 17
Chapter 2: Crafting a Winning Social Media Strategy 23
    Understanding Your Audience 23
    Setting Clear Objectives 28
    Choosing the Right Platforms 33
    Creating a Content Plan 38
Chapter 3: Creating Compelling Content 43
    Content Types and Formats 43
    Storytelling Techniques 49
    Visual Branding 54
    User-Generated Content 60
Chapter 4: Leveraging Influencer Marketing 66
    Finding the Right Influencers 66
    Building Authentic Partnerships 72
    Measuring Influencer Impact 76
    Navigating Challenges 81
Chapter 5: Engaging Your Audience 87
    Building Community 87

Interactive Content 92
Responding to Feedback 96
Managing Negative Feedback 102
Chapter 6: Data-Driven Social Media Marketing 107
Understanding Social Media Analytics 107
Tools for Data Analysis 112
Making Data-Driven Decisions 117
Predictive Analytics 122
Chapter 7: Paid Advertising Strategies 128
Introduction to Social Media Ads 128
Creating Effective Ad Campaigns 134
Budgeting and Bidding 140
Measuring Ad Performance 144
Chapter 8: Automation and Efficiency 150
Social Media Management Tools 150
Creating an Automated Workflow 156
Maintaining Human Touch 161
Review and Optimization 165
Chapter 9: Adapting to Platform Changes 171
Keeping Up with Algorithm Updates 171
Adapting Content Strategy 175
Testing and Experimentation 180
Learning from Success and Failure 186
Chapter 10: Future Trends in Social Media Marketing 192
The Role of AI and Machine Learning 192
Evolving Consumer Behaviors 197
Sustainable and Ethical Marketing 202

Conclusion..208

Introduction

In today's fast-paced digital world, social media has become an indispensable part of our lives. From connecting with friends and family to discovering new products and services, social media platforms are where people spend a significant portion of their time. For businesses, this presents an incredible opportunity to reach and engage with potential customers like never before. However, with great opportunity comes great competition, and to stand out in the crowded digital landscape, mastering social media marketing is essential.

This book is your guide to navigating this dynamic and ever-evolving field, aims to equip you with the knowledge and tools you need to harness the full potential of social media marketing. Whether you're a seasoned marketer looking to stay ahead of the curve or a newcomer eager to make your mark, the strategies and insights shared in these pages will help you achieve your goals.

The journey begins with understanding the evolution of social media marketing. By exploring its origins and the significant shifts that have occurred over the years, you'll gain a solid foundation for why social media is such a powerful marketing tool today. From there, we'll dive into crafting a winning social media strategy, where you'll learn how to identify your audience, set clear objectives, and create a content plan that resonates.

Creating compelling content is at the heart of any successful social media campaign. We'll delve into the art of storytelling, the importance of visual branding, and the power of user-generated content. By mastering these elements, you'll be able to create posts that not only capture attention but also drive meaningful engagement.

Influencer marketing has emerged as a game-changer in recent years, and dedicating a chapter to this topic will show you how to find the right influencers, build authentic partnerships, and measure the impact of your campaigns. Engaging your audience is another critical component of social media success, and we'll explore strategies for building a community, interacting with followers, and managing feedback effectively.

Data-driven decision-making is a recurring theme throughout this book. By understanding social media analytics and using the right tools, you can continuously refine your strategy and improve your results. We'll also cover paid advertising strategies, from creating effective ad campaigns to managing your budget and measuring performance.

Efficiency is key in social media marketing, and automation can help you streamline your efforts while maintaining a personal touch. We'll discuss the best tools for automation, how to create workflows, and the importance of continuous review and optimization.

The social media landscape is constantly changing, and staying adaptable is crucial. We'll guide you through keeping up with platform updates, adjusting your content strategy, and learning from both successes and failures. Finally, we'll look ahead to future trends, including the role of AI, evolving consumer behaviors, and the importance of sustainable and ethical marketing practices.

Throughout this book, you'll find practical advice, real-world examples, and actionable strategies designed to help you master social media marketing. The goal is not just to keep up with the latest trends but to stay ahead and achieve unstoppable growth. Let's embark on this journey together and unlock the full potential of social media marketing.

Chapter 1: The Evolution of Social Media Marketing

The Dawn of Social Media

At the turn of the millennium, the world witnessed a seismic shift in how people communicate. The advent of social media platforms revolutionized the very fabric of social interaction. Websites like Friendster and MySpace emerged as pioneers, offering users a new way to connect and share their lives online. These platforms were more than just digital meeting places; they were the harbingers of a new era where the virtual and the real began to intertwine.

The early 2000s were marked by a sense of novelty and excitement. For the first time, people could create profiles, upload photos, and share their thoughts with a global audience. The boundaries of geography and time dissolved, fostering connections that would have been impossible in the pre-digital age. This newfound connectivity brought about a profound change in personal relationships, but it also laid the groundwork for what would become a marketing revolution.

The Birth of a Digital Society

As social media gained traction, it quickly became clear that these platforms were more than just social networks; they were forming the backbone of a new digital society. Sites like Facebook, which launched in 2004, and Twitter, which followed in 2006, introduced features that encouraged not just connection, but interaction on a scale previously unimaginable. Facebook's "News Feed" and Twitter's real-time updates created dynamic, ever-evolving digital landscapes.

This shift had profound implications for marketing. Traditional advertising methods, which relied heavily on one-way communication, were suddenly inadequate. Businesses began to realize that social media offered a unique opportunity to engage with consumers in a more personal and immediate way. The concept of a passive audience was replaced by the notion of an active community, where feedback was instantaneous and public.

The Power of User-Generated Content

One of the most significant developments in the early days of social media was the rise of user-generated content. Platforms like YouTube, which launched in 2005, empowered individuals to become content creators. This democratization of content creation meant that anyone with an internet connection could share their videos, thoughts, and ideas with the world.

User-generated content transformed the marketing landscape. It shifted the power dynamics, allowing consumers to shape brand narratives in ways that were previously impossible. Brands began to understand the value of authenticity and the importance of engaging with their audience on a more personal level. Influencer marketing emerged as a powerful tool, leveraging the reach and credibility of individuals who had built substantial followings through their own content.

The Early Innovators

Several early adopters understood the potential of social media and began to experiment with creative ways to reach their audiences. For instance, Coca-Cola's "MyCokeRewards" program in the mid-2000s used social media to engage customers and encourage them to share their experiences online. Similarly, Nike's use of social media to promote its "Nike+ Running" app demonstrated the power of integrating digital technology with fitness and community building.

These early innovators set the stage for the sophisticated strategies we see today. They understood that social media was not just another marketing channel; it was a new paradigm that required a different approach. Their willingness to experiment and adapt laid the foundation for the modern social media marketing landscape.

A New Marketing Paradigm

The dawn of social media marked the beginning of a new marketing paradigm. It was no longer sufficient to broadcast messages to a passive audience. Instead, brands had to learn to listen, engage, and respond. This new approach required a deep understanding of the audience and a commitment to creating genuine connections.

The evolution of social media from simple networking sites to powerful marketing tools was swift and transformative. It challenged traditional notions of advertising and opened up a world of possibilities for brands willing to embrace change. As we look back on the early days of social media, it's clear that this period was just the beginning of a revolution that continues to shape the way we communicate and connect today.

In this digital society, the lines between personal and professional, consumer and creator, are increasingly blurred. Social media has not only changed the way we interact but also redefined the very nature of community and connection. As we move forward, the lessons learned from the dawn of social media will continue to inform and inspire the strategies of tomorrow.

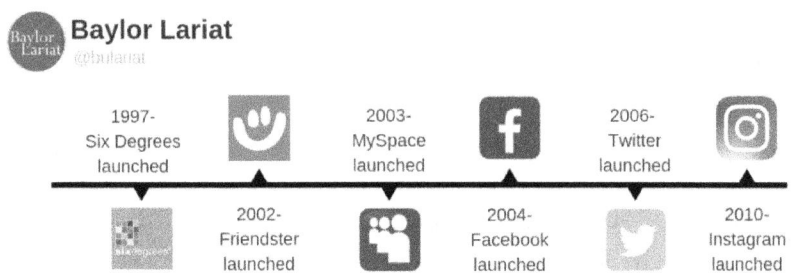

The Dawn of Social Media Platforms. Source: baylorlariat.com

The Rise of Platforms

The digital age has witnessed the meteoric rise of social media platforms, transforming the way we communicate, consume content, and connect with brands. These platforms have not only reshaped our social interactions but have also revolutionized marketing strategies. Understanding the evolution of these platforms and their unique characteristics is crucial for leveraging their full potential in your social media marketing efforts.

Facebook: The Pioneer of Social Connectivity

When Facebook launched in 2004, it marked the beginning of a new era in social media. Initially designed as a networking site for college students, Facebook quickly expanded its reach to a global audience. Its user-friendly interface and innovative features, such as the News Feed and Like button, made it a popular choice for users of all ages.

For marketers, Facebook offered an unprecedented opportunity to reach a vast audience. Its powerful advertising platform allows for highly targeted campaigns based on user demographics, interests, and behaviors. Brands can create dedicated pages, engage with followers, and use insights to refine their strategies. Facebook's continued innovation, including the integration of e-commerce features and live streaming, ensures it remains a vital tool for marketers.

X (formerly Twitter): Real-Time Conversations

Launched in 2006, X introduced a new way of sharing information through short, real-time updates. Its 140-character limit (now 280) forced users to be concise and creative, leading to the rise of hashtags and trending topics. The platform's fast-paced nature makes it an ideal space for real-time engagement, news dissemination, and customer service.

For marketers, X offers a unique space to join conversations, engage with followers, and stay on top of industry trends. Brands can use X to provide timely updates, handle customer inquiries, and build a personality through witty and relevant posts. The platform's advertising options, including promoted posts and trends, enable targeted outreach to specific audiences.

Instagram: Visual Storytelling

Instagram, which debuted in 2010, capitalized on the growing popularity of visual content. Its emphasis on photos and short videos, enhanced by filters and editing tools, made it a favorite among users looking to share their lives creatively. Instagram's Stories feature, inspired by Snapchat, further increased user engagement with ephemeral content.

Marketers quickly recognized Instagram's potential for visual storytelling. Brands use Instagram to showcase products, behind-the-scenes content, and user-generated photos. The platform's shopping features allow users to purchase products directly from posts, blending social interaction with e-commerce. Influencer marketing thrives on Instagram, with partnerships that reach engaged and visually-oriented audiences.

LinkedIn: Professional Networking

LinkedIn, launched in 2003, carved out a niche as the go-to platform for professional networking. Initially focused on job seekers and recruiters, LinkedIn has evolved into a robust platform for industry news, thought leadership, and B2B marketing. Its professional tone and extensive user profiles make it a valuable resource for networking and career development.

For marketers, LinkedIn offers opportunities to connect with industry professionals, share expert content, and generate leads. Company pages and LinkedIn groups facilitate community building and engagement within specific industries. Sponsored content and InMail provide targeted advertising options, reaching decision-makers and professionals.

YouTube: Video Dominance

YouTube, launched in 2005, revolutionized video content consumption and creation. As the world's largest video-sharing platform, YouTube offers a vast library of content ranging from tutorials to entertainment. Its monetization options, including ads and channel memberships, have created new revenue streams for content creators.

Marketers leverage YouTube to reach audiences through engaging video content. Tutorials, product demos, and vlogs allow brands to connect with viewers in an informative and entertaining way. YouTube's advertising platform enables precise targeting based on user interests and viewing habits, making it a powerful tool for video marketing.

TikTok: The New Contender

TikTok, the latest entrant in the social media arena, has quickly gained popularity, especially among younger audiences. Launched in 2016, TikTok's short-form video format, combined with creative editing tools and viral challenges, has captured the imagination of users worldwide. Its algorithm-driven feed ensures content discovery and engagement.

For marketers, TikTok represents an opportunity to reach a highly engaged and trend-savvy audience. Brands can create fun, authentic content that resonates with TikTok's playful and creative user base. Influencer collaborations and hashtag challenges are popular strategies for increasing brand visibility and engagement on the platform.

As social media platforms continue to evolve, staying informed about their unique features and user demographics is essential for effective marketing. Each platform offers distinct opportunities and challenges, and understanding these nuances allows you to craft strategies that resonate with your target audience. By leveraging the strengths of each platform, you can maximize your reach and achieve unstoppable growth in the ever-changing digital landscape.

The Shift to Engagement

In the early days of social media, brands approached these platforms much like traditional media channels. They broadcasted their messages, hoping to reach as many people as possible. This one-way communication mirrored the tactics used in television and print advertising. However, as social media matured, it became clear that this method was missing a critical component: interaction.

The real power of social media lies in its ability to foster two-way communication. Unlike traditional media, social platforms invite users to comment, share, and engage in dialogue. This shift from broadcasting to conversation has fundamentally changed the nature of marketing. Brands are no longer distant entities speaking at consumers; they are participants in an ongoing, dynamic exchange.

The Importance of Authentic Engagement

Authentic engagement goes beyond simply responding to comments or liking posts. It involves creating meaningful interactions that resonate with your audience. Consumers today crave authenticity and transparency. They want to feel connected to brands on a personal level and are quick to recognize insincerity.

Take, for instance, the rise of live streaming. Platforms like Facebook Live and Instagram Live have given brands the ability to connect with their audience in real-time. These live interactions create a sense of immediacy and intimacy, breaking down barriers and fostering a deeper connection. Brands that embrace this level of engagement can build loyalty and trust more effectively than those that stick to traditional, impersonal methods.

The Role of Community Management

Community management has emerged as a critical component of social media strategy. Effective community managers are not just social media moderators; they are brand ambassadors who embody the brand's voice and values. They engage with followers, address concerns, and facilitate conversations that strengthen the community.

A prime example of successful community management is Wendy's X account. Known for its witty and sometimes snarky interactions, Wendy's has built a strong social media presence by engaging with followers in a fun and authentic manner. This approach has not only increased brand visibility but also fostered a loyal and engaged community.

User-Generated Content and Brand Advocacy

User-generated content (UGC) has become a cornerstone of modern social media marketing. Encouraging your audience to create and share content related to your brand can amplify your reach and enhance engagement. UGC adds an element of authenticity and trust, as content created by real users is often perceived as more genuine than brand-produced content.

Campaigns that successfully leverage UGC can generate significant buzz and engagement. For example, the #ShareaCoke campaign by Coca-Cola invited customers to find bottles with their names on them, share photos on social media, and use the hashtag. This simple yet effective strategy turned customers into brand advocates, generating millions of social media impressions and fostering a sense of community.

Metrics That Matter: Measuring Engagement

As the focus has shifted to engagement, so too has the way we measure success on social media. Traditional metrics like reach and impressions are still important, but they don't tell the whole story. Engagement metrics such as likes, comments, shares, and direct messages provide deeper insights into how your audience is interacting with your content.

High engagement rates indicate that your content is resonating with your audience and prompting them to take action. Analyzing these metrics helps brands understand what types of content drive the most interaction and how they can adjust their strategies accordingly.

Building Lasting Relationships

Ultimately, the shift to engagement is about building lasting relationships with your audience. Social media is not just a platform for promoting products or services; it's a space for creating meaningful connections. Brands that prioritize engagement are better positioned to foster loyalty and trust, which can lead to long-term success.

This new era of social media marketing demands a different approach—one that values interaction, authenticity, and community. By embracing these principles, brands can create vibrant, engaged communities that drive not just business growth, but also a deeper, more personal connection with their audience.

Current Trends

The landscape of social media marketing is dynamic, constantly evolving to adapt to new technologies, consumer behaviors, and market demands. Staying ahead of these trends is crucial for any marketer aiming to maintain relevance and drive growth. Here, we explore some of the most significant trends shaping the industry today, providing insights and strategies to help you leverage these developments effectively.

The Shift to Short-Form Video

One of the most prominent trends in social media marketing is the rise of short-form video content. Platforms like TikTok have popularized this format, encouraging users to create and share brief, engaging videos. Instagram's Reels and YouTube Shorts have followed suit, further cementing the trend.

Short-form videos are effective because they cater to the decreasing attention spans of modern audiences. These videos are easily consumable, shareable, and often viral in nature. For marketers, this means creating content that is not only visually appealing but also quick to deliver a message or evoke an emotion. Tips, tricks, behind-the-scenes looks, and quick product demonstrations are all excellent ways to utilize short-form video.

The Rise of Social Commerce

Social commerce, or the direct selling of products through social media platforms, is transforming the way consumers shop online. Instagram, Facebook, and Pinterest have integrated shopping features, allowing users to purchase products without leaving the app. This seamless shopping experience is becoming increasingly popular, particularly among younger demographics who prefer convenient, integrated shopping options.

For businesses, social commerce offers a unique opportunity to convert social media engagement into sales. Creating shoppable posts, leveraging influencer partnerships for authentic endorsements, and using targeted ads to reach potential buyers are effective strategies to capitalize on this trend. Additionally, integrating user-generated content showcasing products in real-life scenarios can build trust and drive sales.

Authenticity and Transparency

Consumers today crave authenticity and transparency from the brands they follow. This trend has led to a shift in how companies approach social media marketing. Instead of overly polished and curated content, there is a growing preference for genuine, relatable, and behind-the-scenes content that humanizes brands.

Marketers can harness this trend by being more open and honest in their communications. Sharing stories about the company's values, mission, and the people behind the brand can create a deeper connection with the audience. Live videos, employee takeovers, and unfiltered posts are great ways to showcase authenticity. Additionally, addressing mistakes openly and showing the company's response to feedback can build trust and loyalty.

Influencer Partnerships

While influencer marketing is not new, its evolution and the increasing importance of micro and nano-influencers mark a significant trend. These smaller-scale influencers often have highly engaged and loyal followers, making them valuable partners for brands looking to reach niche audiences authentically.

Collaborating with influencers who align with your brand values and target audience can amplify your message and enhance credibility. Instead of focusing solely on follower count, consider engagement rates and the influencer's ability to create compelling content. Long-term partnerships are also more effective, as they allow for deeper integration and more authentic endorsements.

Data Privacy and Ethical Marketing

With growing concerns over data privacy, social media platforms and marketers are under increased scrutiny. Consumers are more aware of how their data is being used and are demanding greater transparency and control. This has led to stricter regulations and a push towards more ethical marketing practices.

For marketers, this trend underscores the importance of respecting consumer privacy and being transparent about data collection and usage. Implementing robust data protection measures, being clear about how data is used, and obtaining explicit consent are critical steps. Moreover, focusing on building genuine relationships with customers rather than relying solely on data-driven targeting can foster trust and loyalty.

The Integration of AI and Automation

Artificial intelligence (AI) and automation are transforming social media marketing by enabling more efficient and personalized interactions. AI-powered tools can analyze vast amounts of data to provide insights, predict trends, and automate tasks like content scheduling and customer service.

Marketers can leverage AI to enhance their strategies in various ways. Chatbots, for example, can provide instant customer support, improving response times and user satisfaction. Predictive analytics can help in tailoring content to user preferences, increasing engagement rates. Automating routine tasks frees up time for more strategic activities, allowing marketers to focus on creativity and innovation.

Staying ahead of these trends requires a proactive approach and a willingness to adapt. By embracing short-form video, social commerce, authenticity, influencer partnerships, data privacy, and AI, you can ensure your social media marketing efforts remain relevant and effective in an ever-changing digital landscape.

Chapter 2: Crafting a Winning Social Media Strategy

Understanding Your Audience

Understanding your audience is the cornerstone of any successful social media marketing strategy. It goes beyond basic demographics, delving into the nuances of what drives your audience's behaviors, preferences, and needs. By truly knowing who your audience is, you can tailor your content, messaging, and campaigns to resonate more deeply and foster genuine connections.

The Power of Social Listening

Social listening is a powerful tool for gaining insights into your audience. It involves monitoring social media channels for mentions of your brand, competitors, and relevant keywords. This real-time feedback allows you to understand what your audience is talking about, their pain points, and what they value.

By paying attention to these conversations, you can identify trends and shifts in sentiment that can inform your marketing strategy. For example, if you notice a recurring complaint about a particular feature of your product, you can address it directly in your content or even make changes to improve the user experience. Social listening provides a dynamic way to stay attuned to your audience's needs and preferences.

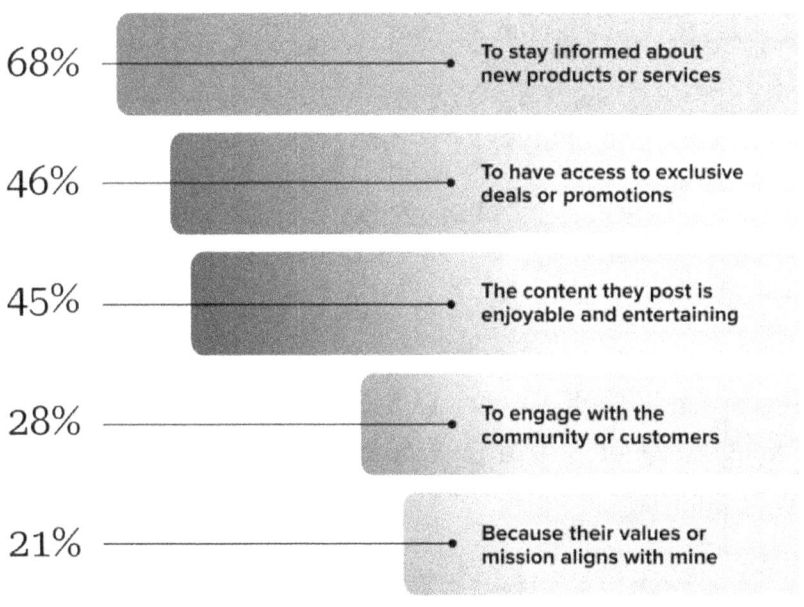

Top Reasons Consumers Follow Brands on Social Media. Source: sproutsocial.com

Creating Detailed Buyer Personas

Buyer personas are semi-fictional representations of your ideal customers based on data and research. They help you visualize your audience and understand their motivations, challenges, and goals. Creating detailed personas involves gathering information from various sources, including customer surveys, interviews, and analytics.

Consider factors such as age, gender, location, interests, and purchasing behavior. But go deeper by exploring their values, lifestyle choices, and what influences their decisions. For instance, if your brand targets young professionals, a persona might be "Tech-Savvy Taylor," a 28-year-old marketing manager who values convenience, innovation, and sustainability.

These personas guide your content creation, ensuring that your messaging speaks directly to the needs and desires of your target audience. When your audience feels understood, they are more likely to engage with your content and develop a loyalty to your brand.

Leveraging Analytics for Insights

Analytics tools provide a wealth of data that can help you understand your audience's behavior on social media. Platforms like Facebook Insights, X Analytics, and Google Analytics offer detailed information about who is engaging with your content, when they are online, and what types of posts they prefer.

For example, you might discover that your audience engages more with video content than with blog posts, or that they are most active in the evenings. These insights allow you to optimize your content strategy, posting schedule, and even the format of your content to better align with your audience's preferences.

Engaging Directly with Your Audience

Direct engagement with your audience can provide valuable insights that data alone cannot offer. Encourage feedback through comments, direct messages, and interactive content like polls and surveys. Ask open-ended questions to understand their opinions and experiences.

Hosting Q&A sessions or live streams can also create opportunities for real-time interaction, allowing you to address questions and gather insights simultaneously. This direct engagement not only helps you understand your audience better but also strengthens the relationship between your brand and its followers.

Observing Competitors

Analyzing your competitors can also provide insights into your shared audience. Observe what type of content resonates with their followers, which posts get the most engagement, and how they interact with their audience. This can highlight gaps in your own strategy and inspire new approaches to engage your audience more effectively.

However, it's important to differentiate your brand and not just mimic competitors. Use these insights to innovate and offer something unique that sets you apart in the eyes of your audience.

Continual Learning and Adaptation

Understanding your audience is not a one-time task; it's an ongoing process. As social media and consumer behaviors evolve, so too should your understanding of your audience. Regularly update your personas, stay active in social listening, and adapt your strategies based on the latest insights.

By committing to continual learning and adaptation, you can ensure that your marketing efforts remain relevant and effective, fostering deeper connections and driving long-term success. The more you understand your audience, the better equipped you are to meet their needs and exceed their expectations, ultimately leading to a more engaged and loyal following.

Setting Clear Objectives

Setting clear objectives is the cornerstone of any successful social media marketing strategy. Without well-defined goals, it's easy to get lost in the sea of metrics and lose sight of what you're trying to achieve. Clear objectives not only provide direction but also enable you to measure your progress and adjust your strategies as needed. Here's how to set objectives that will drive your social media marketing efforts towards success.

Defining Your Purpose

Before diving into specific goals, it's essential to understand your broader purpose for being on social media. Are you looking to increase brand awareness, drive website traffic, generate leads, or boost sales? Each of these purposes requires a different approach and set of metrics. By clearly defining your purpose, you can tailor your objectives to align with your overall business goals.

For instance, a brand looking to increase awareness might focus on metrics such as reach and impressions, while a company aiming to boost sales will pay closer attention to conversion rates and revenue generated from social media campaigns.

SMART Goals

One of the most effective ways to set clear objectives is to use the SMART framework, which stands for Specific, Measurable, Achievable, Relevant, and Time-bound. This method ensures that your goals are well-defined and realistic, making them easier to achieve.

- **Specific**: Your objectives should be clear and specific. Instead of a vague goal like "increase engagement," aim for something precise, such as "increase engagement on Instagram posts by 20% over the next three months."

- **Measurable**: To track your progress, your goals must be measurable. This means defining what success looks like in numerical terms, such as "gain 1,000 new followers on X in the next quarter."

- **Achievable**: While it's good to be ambitious, your goals should also be attainable. Setting unrealistic objectives can lead to frustration and burnout. Consider your current resources and constraints when setting your goals.

- **Relevant**: Ensure that your objectives align with your overall business goals. For example, if your primary business goal is to expand into new markets, your social media objectives might focus on increasing followers and engagement from those specific regions.

- **Time-bound**: Every goal should have a deadline. This creates a sense of urgency and helps you stay focused. For example, "increase website traffic from social media by 30% within six months."

SMART Goals Framework. Source: freepik.com

Breaking Down Goals into Actionable Steps

Once you've set your SMART goals, break them down into smaller, actionable steps. This makes it easier to manage your efforts and track progress. For instance, if your goal is to increase engagement, actionable steps might include posting more frequently, experimenting with different types of content, and actively responding to comments and messages.

Each step should have its own mini-goal that contributes to the larger objective. This approach not only makes your goals more manageable but also allows you to celebrate small victories along the way, keeping your team motivated and focused.

Monitoring and Adjusting

Setting clear objectives is not a one-time task. It requires continuous monitoring and adjustment based on your results and any changes in your business environment or social media platforms. Use analytics tools to track your progress and gather insights into what's working and what's not. If you find that certain strategies aren't delivering the desired results, be prepared to pivot and try new approaches.

Regularly reviewing your objectives and performance ensures that you stay on track and make informed decisions. It also helps you identify opportunities for improvement and innovation, allowing you to stay ahead in the competitive social media landscape.

Clear objectives are the foundation of effective social media marketing. They provide direction, enable measurement, and ensure that your efforts are aligned with your overall business goals. By defining your purpose, setting SMART goals, breaking them down into actionable steps, and continuously monitoring and adjusting your strategies, you can achieve significant and sustainable success in your social media marketing endeavors.

Choosing the Right Platforms

Selecting the right social media platforms is a crucial step in crafting an effective social media strategy. Not all platforms are created equal, and each has its unique audience, strengths, and challenges. Choosing the right ones ensures that your content reaches the most relevant audience and achieves the desired impact.

Knowing Your Audience

The first step in selecting the right platforms is understanding where your audience spends their time. Different demographics gravitate towards different platforms. For example, Instagram and TikTok are popular among younger audiences, while LinkedIn is the go-to for professionals and B2B interactions. Researching your target audience's habits and preferences will guide you to the platforms where your efforts will be most effective.

Consider conducting surveys, leveraging analytics from your existing platforms, and studying industry reports to gather data on your audience's social media behavior. This insight will help you make informed decisions about where to focus your efforts.

Platform Strengths and Features

Each social media platform has distinct features and content types that perform well. Understanding these can help you match your content with the right platform:

- **Facebook**: Versatile with a wide range of content types including text, images, videos, and live streams. Ideal for community building and engaging a broad audience.

- **Instagram**: Highly visual, best for images, short videos, and stories. Great for brands with strong visual content and those targeting younger demographics.

- **X**: Fast-paced and text-heavy, perfect for real-time updates, news, and short, impactful messages. Useful for brands that can engage in ongoing conversations.

- **LinkedIn**: Professional network ideal for B2B marketing, industry news, and professional content. Best for brands targeting professionals and businesses.

- **TikTok**: Short-form video content that appeals to a younger audience. Effective for creative, engaging, and viral content.

- **Pinterest**: Image-centric and highly visual, great for lifestyle, DIY, and e-commerce brands. Useful for driving traffic through visually appealing pins.

Understanding these strengths allows you to tailor your content strategy to fit the platform, enhancing your engagement and effectiveness.

Aligning with Your Goals

Your choice of platforms should also align with your business goals. If your goal is to increase brand awareness, platforms with a broad reach like Facebook and Instagram might be suitable. For driving website traffic, Pinterest and LinkedIn can be highly effective. If you aim to engage directly with customers and build a community, consider platforms like X and Facebook.

Define your primary objectives clearly. Whether it's brand awareness, lead generation, customer engagement, or sales, your goals will help determine which platforms are best suited to achieve them.

Resource Allocation

Managing multiple social media platforms requires time, effort, and resources. It's better to be active and effective on a few platforms than to spread yourself too thin across many. Assess your team's capacity and resources before committing to new platforms. Consistent, high-quality content and timely engagement are crucial for success on any platform.

Staying Updated with Trends

The social media landscape is constantly evolving. New platforms emerge, and existing ones change their features and algorithms. Staying updated with these trends can give you an edge. For instance, the rise of video content has made platforms like TikTok and Instagram Reels immensely popular. Being an early adopter of emerging trends can help you stand out and capture new audience segments.

Testing and Analyzing

Choosing the right platforms isn't a one-time decision; it's an ongoing process. Regularly review your analytics to assess the performance of your chosen platforms. Are you meeting your engagement and conversion goals? Are there new platforms gaining popularity with your target audience?

Don't hesitate to experiment with new platforms and content types. Testing different approaches and analyzing the results will provide valuable insights into what works best for your brand.

Making Strategic Decisions

Ultimately, choosing the right platforms is about making strategic decisions based on data, goals, and available resources. By understanding your audience, leveraging platform strengths, aligning with your objectives, and staying adaptable, you can create a focused and effective social media strategy. This approach ensures that your efforts are not only seen but also resonate with the right people, driving meaningful engagement and results.

Creating a Content Plan

A well-crafted content plan is the backbone of any successful social media strategy. It ensures that your content is consistent, relevant, and aligned with your marketing goals. By planning your content in advance, you can maintain a steady stream of engaging posts that keep your audience interested and coming back for more. Here's how to create a content plan that will set you up for success.

Defining Your Content Goals

Before you start planning your content, it's essential to define your goals. What do you want to achieve with your social media content? Common goals include increasing brand awareness, driving traffic to your website, generating leads, or boosting engagement. Your goals will guide the type of content you create and how you measure its success.

For instance, if your goal is to increase brand awareness, you might focus on content that highlights your brand's story, values, and unique selling points. If you aim to drive traffic to your website, you could create posts that feature blog excerpts, product highlights, or promotional offers with clear calls-to-action.

Choosing Content Themes and Topics

To keep your content varied and interesting, it's helpful to establish a few core themes and topics. These should align with your brand and resonate with your audience. Themes can include educational content, behind-the-scenes glimpses, user-generated content, industry news, and promotional posts.

Within these themes, brainstorm specific topics that you can develop into posts. For example, under the educational theme, you could create how-to guides, tips and tricks, and case studies. For behind-the-scenes content, you might share stories about your team, office culture, or the production process.

Developing a Content Calendar

A content calendar is a crucial tool for organizing and scheduling your posts. It helps you maintain consistency and ensures that you cover all your themes and topics. Start by mapping out the frequency of your posts. How often will you post on each platform? This depends on your audience's preferences and the nature of each platform.

Once you've determined the posting frequency, fill in your calendar with specific posts. Include the date, platform, content theme, topic, and any accompanying media such as images, videos, or links. Planning your content in advance allows you to see the big picture and ensures a balanced mix of different types of posts.

Creating and Curating Content

With your calendar in place, it's time to start creating and curating content. Creating original content is essential for showcasing your brand's voice and expertise. This includes writing blog posts, designing graphics, producing videos, and taking photos. Ensure that all content is high-quality and aligns with your brand's style and tone.

In addition to creating content, consider curating content from other sources. Sharing relevant articles, infographics, and videos from industry leaders can provide value to your audience and position your brand as a knowledgeable resource. Just make sure to credit the original source and add your own commentary to personalize the post.

Engaging with Your Audience

Posting content is just the beginning. Engaging with your audience is crucial for building relationships and fostering a sense of community. Respond to comments, answer questions, and encourage discussions. Use your content to start conversations and show that you value your audience's input.

Engagement also involves monitoring your content's performance. Use analytics tools to track metrics such as likes, shares, comments, and click-through rates. This data provides insights into what types of content resonate most with your audience and helps you refine your strategy over time.

Adapting and Optimizing Your Plan

A successful content plan is not static. It requires continuous adaptation and optimization based on your audience's feedback and your content's performance. Regularly review your analytics to identify trends and adjust your plan accordingly. Experiment with different types of content, posting times, and formats to see what works best.

Stay flexible and be ready to pivot when necessary. Social media trends and algorithms change frequently, and being able to adapt your content plan will keep you ahead of the curve. By staying responsive to your audience's needs and the evolving digital landscape, you can maintain a dynamic and effective social media presence.

Creating a content plan involves understanding your audience, defining your goals, choosing themes, developing a calendar, creating and curating content, engaging with your audience, and continuously adapting. This structured approach ensures that your social media efforts are strategic, consistent, and impactful. By following these steps, you can create a content plan that not only engages your audience but also drives meaningful results for your business.

Chapter 3: Creating Compelling Content

Content Types and Formats

Creating engaging content for social media is both an art and a science. The variety of content types and formats available allows brands to connect with their audience in numerous ways, catering to different preferences and behaviors. Understanding the strengths and best practices for each type can help you craft a dynamic and effective content strategy.

Visual Content: The Power of Images and Infographics

Visual content is a cornerstone of social media. Images and infographics are highly shareable and can convey complex information quickly and effectively. High-quality images grab attention and can tell a story at a glance, making them ideal for platforms like Instagram, Pinterest, and Facebook.

Infographics, on the other hand, are excellent for breaking down data and presenting it in an easily digestible format. They combine visuals with key information, making them perfect for explaining complex ideas or statistics. Infographics work well on platforms like LinkedIn, where educational content is valued.

The Rise of Video Content

Video content has seen a meteoric rise in popularity across all social media platforms. From short, engaging clips on TikTok and Instagram Reels to longer, in-depth videos on YouTube and Facebook, video is an incredibly versatile format.

Short-form videos are great for quick tips, product showcases, and behind-the-scenes looks. They cater to the fast-paced nature of social media consumption. Longer videos, such as tutorials, interviews, and webinars, allow for more detailed storytelling and engagement. Live streaming adds another layer, providing real-time interaction and a sense of immediacy that can be incredibly engaging for viewers.

Stories: Ephemeral Content with Lasting Impact

Stories, popularized by Snapchat and adopted by Instagram and Facebook, are short, temporary posts that disappear after 24 hours. This format creates a sense of urgency and exclusivity, encouraging users to check in regularly.

Stories are perfect for sharing updates, promoting limited-time offers, or giving a behind-the-scenes look at your brand. Their ephemeral nature makes them feel more personal and spontaneous, fostering a closer connection with your audience. Interactive elements like polls, quizzes, and question stickers can further boost engagement.

Text-Based Content: The Power of Words

While visuals dominate social media, text-based content still plays a crucial role. Thought-provoking quotes, engaging captions, and informative blog posts can drive significant engagement, especially on platforms like X and LinkedIn.

X thrives on short, impactful messages and real-time updates, making it ideal for sharing news, insights, and engaging in conversations. LinkedIn is perfect for long-form articles, industry insights, and professional updates. Well-crafted text-based content can establish your brand as a thought leader and drive meaningful interactions.

User-Generated Content: Building Community and Trust

User-generated content (UGC) leverages the creativity and advocacy of your audience. Encouraging your followers to create and share content related to your brand can significantly enhance your reach and credibility. UGC can take many forms, including photos, videos, reviews, and testimonials.

Campaigns that highlight UGC not only showcase genuine user experiences but also foster a sense of community and trust. For example, a brand might run a photo contest where customers share images of themselves using a product, with a branded hashtag to increase visibility.

Interactive Content: Engaging Your Audience

Interactive content, such as polls, quizzes, and contests, actively involves your audience and encourages participation. These formats can boost engagement and provide valuable insights into your audience's preferences and opinions.

For instance, Instagram Stories' interactive features, like polls and questions, allow for direct feedback and engagement. Facebook and LinkedIn also offer poll features that can be used to gather opinions on relevant topics or to generate discussion.

Podcasts: The Audio Revolution

Podcasts have surged in popularity, offering a unique way to engage with your audience through audio content. They provide an opportunity for in-depth discussions, interviews, and storytelling, catering to users who prefer listening over reading or watching.

Podcasts can be shared on various platforms, including Apple Podcasts, Spotify, and directly through social media channels. Promoting podcast episodes with engaging summaries and quotes can drive traffic and expand your reach.

5 Creative Social Media Content Ideas for Brands. Source: socialchamp.io

The Importance of a Balanced Content Strategy

A successful social media strategy leverages a mix of content types and formats to keep the audience engaged and cater to different preferences. Balancing visual, video, text-based, user-generated, interactive, and audio content ensures a dynamic and comprehensive approach.

By understanding the unique strengths of each content type and format, you can create a more engaging and effective social media presence. This diversity not only keeps your audience interested but also allows you to experiment and discover what resonates most with your followers.

Storytelling Techniques

Storytelling is a powerful tool that can captivate your audience, evoke emotions, and create a lasting impression. A well-told story can transform mundane content into something memorable and engaging. Here are some effective storytelling techniques to enhance your social media presence.

Create a Strong Narrative Arc

Every good story has a clear beginning, middle, and end. This structure helps to guide your audience through your narrative seamlessly. Start with a hook that grabs attention. This could be an intriguing question, a surprising fact, or a relatable scenario. Develop your story by introducing challenges or conflicts, and build up to a climax. Finally, provide a resolution that leaves your audience with a takeaway or a call to action.

For example, if you're promoting a new product, start with a common problem your audience faces (beginning), introduce your product as a solution (middle), and end with a real-life success story or testimonials (end).

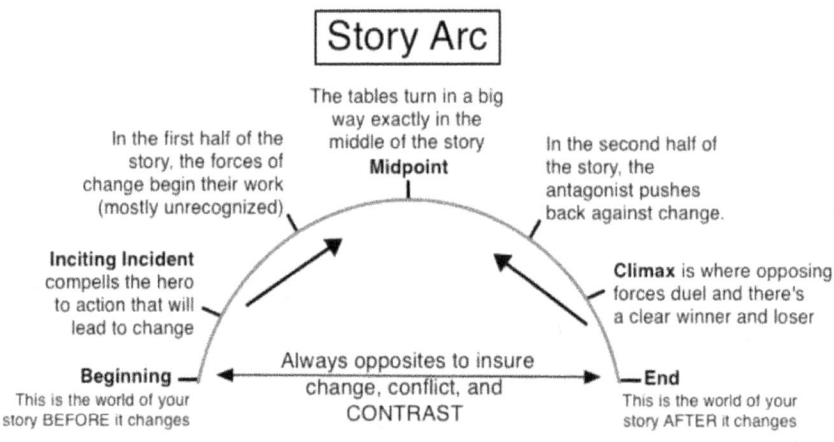

Storytelling Techniques. Source: gonarrative.com

Use Emotion to Connect

Emotions are a powerful driver of engagement. Whether it's joy, sadness, fear, or excitement, tapping into your audience's emotions can make your stories more impactful. Share stories that evoke feelings and make your audience feel something profound. This emotional connection encourages sharing and interaction.

For instance, if you're a nonprofit organization, sharing heartfelt stories about the people you've helped can evoke empathy and motivate your audience to support your cause.

Show, Don't Tell

Visuals are a crucial component of storytelling on social media. Instead of just telling your audience about something, show them. Use photos, videos, infographics, and other visual elements to bring your story to life. A compelling image or video can convey emotions and messages more effectively than words alone.

For example, instead of describing the vibrant atmosphere at your company's event, share a video capturing the highlights, the smiles, and the interactions. This immersive approach helps your audience experience the story firsthand.

Be Authentic

Authenticity is key in building trust and credibility. Share real stories about your brand, employees, and customers. Highlight behind-the-scenes moments, challenges you've overcome, and milestones you've achieved. Authentic stories foster a deeper connection and make your brand more relatable.

For instance, a small business could share the founder's journey, from the initial idea to the struggles of starting up and the joy of achieving the first major milestone. This genuine narrative can inspire and resonate with your audience.

Incorporate User-Generated Content

User-generated content (UGC) is a treasure trove of authentic stories. Encourage your customers to share their experiences with your brand and feature these stories on your social media channels. UGC not only provides social proof but also adds diverse voices and perspectives to your storytelling.

For example, a beauty brand could invite customers to share their makeup looks created with the brand's products. Highlighting these stories showcases real-life applications and builds a community around your brand.

Keep It Simple and Concise

Attention spans on social media are short, so keep your stories simple and to the point. Avoid unnecessary details that could distract from the main message. Focus on delivering a clear and concise story that captures attention quickly and holds it until the end.

For instance, if you're sharing a customer testimonial, highlight the key points: the problem, the solution, and the positive outcome. This straightforward approach ensures your audience gets the message without losing interest.

Use a Consistent Voice and Style

Maintaining a consistent voice and style across your stories reinforces your brand identity. Whether your brand voice is professional, friendly, witty, or inspirational, ensure that your stories reflect this tone. Consistency helps your audience recognize and connect with your brand more easily.

For example, if your brand has a playful and humorous tone, infuse your stories with lighthearted language and fun visuals. This cohesive style strengthens your brand's personality and makes your content more recognizable.

Storytelling on social media is an art that combines understanding your audience, structuring your narrative, evoking emotions, and using visuals effectively. By incorporating these techniques, you can create compelling stories that engage your audience, build connections, and drive meaningful interactions with your brand.

Visual Branding

Visual branding is the practice of creating a cohesive and recognizable image for your brand across all visual materials. It's a critical aspect of your overall brand strategy, as it helps to establish your brand identity and ensures that your audience can instantly recognize your content, no matter where they encounter it. Consistent visuals build trust and familiarity, which are essential for long-term engagement and loyalty.

Elements of Visual Branding

Visual branding encompasses various elements, each playing a significant role in how your brand is perceived. Key components include your logo, color palette, typography, imagery, and overall design style. These elements should be thoughtfully selected and consistently applied to create a unified look and feel.

Your logo is often the first visual element people associate with your brand. It should be simple, memorable, and versatile enough to work across different mediums. The color palette you choose can evoke specific emotions and set the tone for your brand. For instance, blue often conveys trust and professionalism, while red can evoke excitement and urgency.

Typography, or the fonts you use, also contributes to your brand's personality. Whether you choose a classic serif font or a modern sans-serif, your typography should be legible and reflect your brand's style. Imagery, including photos, illustrations, and graphics, should align with your brand's aesthetic and messaging. Consistent use of design elements, such as shapes and patterns, further reinforces your visual identity.

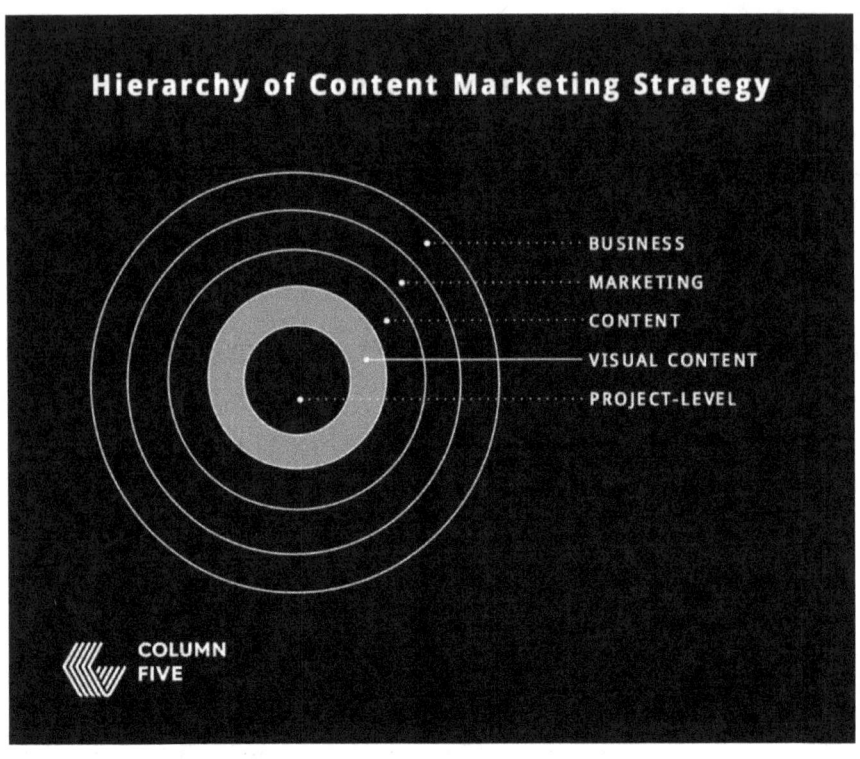

Hierarchy of Content Marketing Strategy. Source: columnfivemedia.com

Crafting a Visual Style Guide

A visual style guide is a document that outlines the rules and standards for your brand's visual elements. It serves as a reference for anyone creating visual content for your brand, ensuring consistency across all platforms and materials. The style guide should include detailed guidelines for your logo usage, color palette, typography, imagery, and any other visual elements specific to your brand.

For example, your style guide should specify how and where your logo can be used, the exact color codes for your brand colors, and the preferred fonts for different types of content. It may also include examples of approved imagery and guidelines for creating new graphics that align with your brand's style. By providing clear and comprehensive guidelines, you can maintain a cohesive visual identity across all touchpoints.

Visual Storytelling

Visual storytelling is a powerful way to connect with your audience on an emotional level. It involves using visual elements to convey a narrative or message, making your content more engaging and memorable. Effective visual storytelling can differentiate your brand and create a deeper connection with your audience.

For instance, a travel brand might use stunning photography and short videos to showcase exotic destinations, evoking a sense of adventure and wanderlust. An eco-friendly brand might use earthy colors and natural imagery to highlight its commitment to sustainability. By aligning your visuals with your brand's story and values, you can create a more compelling and relatable brand experience.

Adapting Visuals for Different Platforms

Different social media platforms have unique requirements and best practices for visual content. Adapting your visuals to fit these specifications is essential for maximizing engagement and maintaining a consistent brand presence.

Instagram, for example, is highly visual and favors high-quality photos and videos. Stories and Reels offer opportunities for creative, ephemeral content that can drive engagement. On Facebook, a mix of images, videos, and graphics works well, while LinkedIn requires a more professional and polished approach.

It's also important to consider the technical specifications for each platform, such as image dimensions and file formats. Ensuring that your visuals are optimized for each platform will improve their appearance and performance, contributing to a better overall user experience.

The Role of Visuals in Building Brand Recognition

Consistent visual branding helps build brand recognition, making it easier for your audience to identify and remember your brand. Over time, your visual elements become associated with your brand's values, personality, and promise. This recognition can lead to increased trust and loyalty, as consumers are more likely to engage with and support brands they are familiar with.

For example, the distinctive color scheme and minimalist design of Apple products are instantly recognizable, conveying a sense of innovation and quality. Similarly, the playful and vibrant visuals used by brands like Coca-Cola and Disney evoke feelings of joy and nostalgia. By investing in consistent and strategic visual branding, you can create a lasting impression that sets your brand apart from the competition.

Evolving Your Visual Branding

While consistency is crucial, it's also important to evolve your visual branding over time to stay relevant and fresh. This doesn't mean overhauling your entire visual identity, but rather making thoughtful updates that reflect changes in your brand, industry trends, and audience preferences.

Regularly reviewing and refining your visual elements ensures that your branding remains effective and resonates with your audience. This might involve updating your color palette, introducing new design elements, or refreshing your logo. By balancing consistency with evolution, you can maintain a strong and relevant visual identity that continues to engage and inspire your audience.

User-Generated Content

User-generated content (UGC) has emerged as a powerful tool in the world of social media marketing. It encompasses any content—such as photos, videos, reviews, and social media posts—created by your customers or followers, rather than by your brand itself. UGC is highly valuable because it provides authentic, relatable, and diverse perspectives on your brand, which can significantly enhance trust and engagement. Here's how to effectively leverage user-generated content to boost your social media strategy.

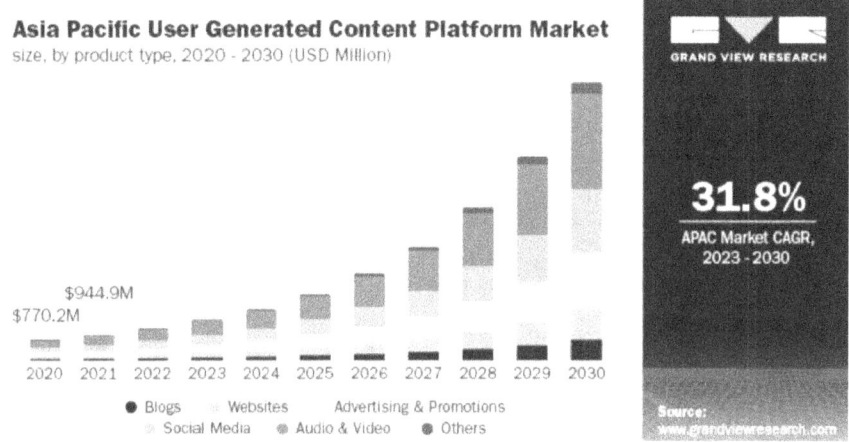

The Growing Market for User-Generated Content in Asia Pacific (2020–2030). Source: grandviewresearch.com

The Power of Authenticity

One of the primary advantages of UGC is its authenticity. In an age where consumers are increasingly skeptical of traditional advertising, content created by real users offers a genuine glimpse into your brand's impact. When potential customers see real people enjoying your products or services, it builds credibility and trust.

Consider a fitness brand that encourages customers to share their workout journeys. Photos and videos of actual users achieving their fitness goals with the brand's products can be far more persuasive than professional ads. This authenticity resonates with audiences, making them more likely to engage with your brand and consider purchasing your products.

Building Community and Engagement

UGC fosters a sense of community among your followers. When customers see their content featured on your social media channels, it creates a feeling of belonging and appreciation. This, in turn, encourages more users to share their experiences, amplifying your brand's reach and engagement.

For instance, a travel company might invite customers to post photos of their adventures using a specific hashtag. Featuring these photos on the company's social media pages not only provides engaging content but also cultivates a community of travel enthusiasts who feel connected to the brand and each other.

Generating Social Proof

Social proof is the psychological phenomenon where people rely on the actions and opinions of others to make decisions. UGC serves as a powerful form of social proof. When potential customers see positive experiences shared by others, it can influence their own purchasing decisions.

Imagine a skincare brand that reposts customer testimonials and before-and-after photos. Seeing real people achieve noticeable results can persuade potential buyers to try the products themselves. This type of content acts as a recommendation from peers, which is often more convincing than traditional marketing messages.

Encouraging Creativity and Participation

UGC campaigns can spark creativity and participation among your audience. By encouraging customers to share their unique perspectives and experiences, you not only gain valuable content but also increase brand loyalty and engagement.

Take, for example, a fashion brand that launches a contest asking followers to style their products in creative ways. Participants can share their looks on social media, tagging the brand for a chance to be featured or win a prize. This not only generates a wealth of diverse content but also drives higher levels of interaction and excitement around the brand.

Showcasing Product Versatility

User-generated content is an excellent way to showcase the versatility of your products. Different users will highlight various features and uses that you might not have considered, providing a broader view of what your products can do.

A tech company, for instance, might see users creating videos demonstrating unique ways to use their gadgets. These diverse applications can appeal to a wider audience, showing potential customers the multiple benefits and functionalities of the products through real-world examples.

How to Encourage User-Generated Content

To effectively harness the power of UGC, it's essential to encourage your audience to participate. Here are a few strategies:

- **Create Branded Hashtags**: Develop unique and catchy hashtags for your campaigns. This makes it easy for users to tag their content and for you to find and curate it.

- **Run Contests and Giveaways**: Incentivize users to share their experiences by offering prizes or features on your social media channels.

- **Feature Customer Stories**: Regularly highlight user-generated content on your profiles. This not only provides you with fresh content but also shows appreciation for your customers.

- **Engage with Your Audience**: Respond to and engage with UGC posts. Acknowledging users' contributions encourages more participation and strengthens community bonds.

User-generated content is a dynamic and effective component of social media marketing. By leveraging the authenticity, community-building, social proof, and creativity that UGC offers, you can enhance your brand's presence and foster deeper connections with your audience. Encourage your customers to share their stories, and watch as their experiences enrich your social media landscape.

Chapter 4: Leveraging Influencer Marketing

Finding the Right Influencers

Before diving into the search for influencers, it's essential to define what you hope to achieve through influencer marketing. Are you looking to increase brand awareness, drive sales, or grow your social media following? Clearly defined goals will help you identify the type of influencers who can best support your objectives.

Consider whether you need macro-influencers with large followings for broad reach or micro-influencers who, despite having smaller audiences, often boast higher engagement rates and niche authority. Your goals will guide your strategy and influence the kind of partnerships you seek.

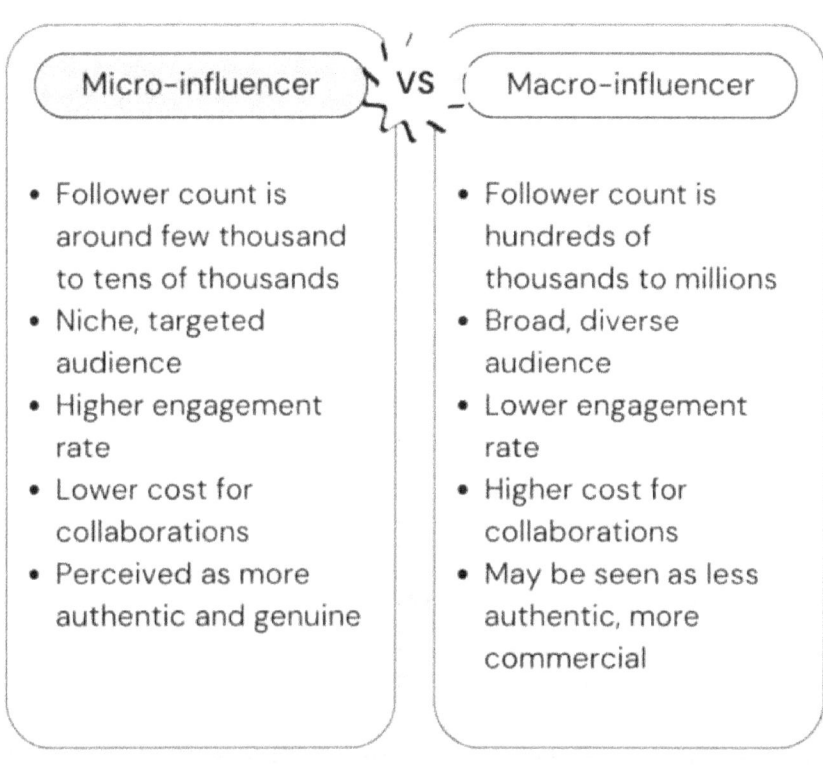

Micro vs. Macro-Influencers. Source: hummingweb.com.au

Understanding Your Target Audience

Knowing your target audience is crucial when selecting influencers. The influencers you choose should resonate with the demographic and psychographic profile of your ideal customers. Look at factors such as age, gender, location, interests, and values. The more aligned an influencer is with your audience, the more authentic and effective the collaboration will be.

Use social media analytics tools to gain insights into your current followers and potential audience. This data will help you identify the types of influencers who are already engaging with similar demographics, ensuring a natural fit for your brand.

Researching Influencer Authenticity

Authenticity is key in influencer marketing. An influencer's credibility and genuine connection with their audience can significantly impact the success of your campaign. Research their previous partnerships and content to ensure they align with your brand values and messaging.

Look for influencers who engage with their followers meaningfully, responding to comments and fostering a sense of community. Authentic influencers tend to have loyal followers who trust their recommendations, which can lead to higher engagement and conversion rates for your campaign.

Evaluating Engagement Metrics

An influencer's follower count is often less important than their engagement rate. High engagement indicates that the influencer's audience is active and interested in their content. Evaluate metrics such as likes, comments, shares, and views to gauge the influencer's impact.

Tools like Social Blade and HypeAuditor can help you analyze an influencer's engagement rates and growth patterns. Look for consistent engagement over time rather than sporadic spikes, which might indicate inauthentic activity. A genuine influencer maintains steady interaction with their audience, reflecting real influence and reach.

Aligning Content Style and Values

The content style and values of the influencer should align with your brand. Review their posts, stories, and overall aesthetic to ensure they match your brand's voice and image. For instance, a fashion brand might look for influencers with a keen sense of style and visually appealing content, while a tech company might seek influencers who provide detailed reviews and insights.

Additionally, consider the influencer's values and how they align with your brand's mission. Collaborating with influencers who share similar values can lead to more authentic partnerships and resonate better with your audience.

Leveraging Influencer Networks and Platforms

There are several platforms and networks designed to connect brands with influencers. Platforms like AspireIQ, Influencity, and Upfluence offer databases of influencers across various niches and allow you to filter by demographics, engagement rates, and more. These tools can streamline the process of finding and reaching out to potential partners.

Explore niche-specific influencer networks as well. For example, if you're in the beauty industry, platforms like Beauty Influencers or Tribe Dynamics can connect you with influencers who specialize in beauty content.

Building Relationships

Building strong relationships with influencers goes beyond transactional interactions. Approach influencers with genuine interest and respect for their work. Personalize your outreach, referencing specific content you admire and explaining why you believe they would be a good fit for your campaign.

Developing long-term relationships with influencers can lead to more authentic and effective collaborations. Consider offering exclusive deals, early access to products, or opportunities to co-create content. These gestures can help build trust and loyalty, resulting in more meaningful partnerships.

Measuring Success and Adaptation

After launching your influencer campaign, it's crucial to measure its success against your defined goals. Track metrics such as engagement, reach, website traffic, and sales conversions. Analyze what worked well and what didn't to refine your strategy for future campaigns.

Be open to adapting your approach based on the results. Influencer marketing is dynamic, and continuous learning and adjustment are essential for long-term success. By staying flexible and responsive, you can maximize the impact of your influencer partnerships and achieve your marketing goals.

Finding the right influencers involves a blend of research, authenticity, and strategic alignment. By focusing on these elements, you can identify influencers who not only enhance your brand's visibility but also foster genuine connections with your target audience. This approach ensures that your influencer marketing efforts are both impactful and sustainable.

Building Authentic Partnerships

In the realm of social media marketing, authentic partnerships with influencers can significantly amplify your brand's reach and credibility. These partnerships, however, need to be genuine and mutually beneficial to be truly effective. Building authentic relationships with influencers requires careful selection, clear communication, and a shared vision. Here's how to create partnerships that resonate and drive results.

Identifying the Right Influencers

The first step in building authentic partnerships is identifying the right influencers. It's not just about the number of followers an influencer has, but rather the relevance of their audience to your brand. Look for influencers whose content, values, and audience align with your brand's mission and target market.

Begin by researching influencers within your niche. Examine their engagement rates, the quality of their content, and their interaction with followers. An influencer with a smaller, highly engaged audience can be more valuable than one with a large but passive following. For example, a fitness brand might seek out personal trainers or fitness enthusiasts who regularly engage with their audience about health and wellness.

Establishing Mutual Goals

Successful partnerships are built on mutual goals and benefits. Before approaching an influencer, clearly define what you hope to achieve from the collaboration. Are you looking to increase brand awareness, drive sales, or boost engagement? Understanding your objectives helps in crafting a proposal that is appealing to both parties.

Engage in open conversations with potential influencers about their goals as well. Discuss how your brand can support their personal brand and audience. A collaboration should feel natural and beneficial for both sides. For instance, a skincare brand might collaborate with a beauty influencer who is passionate about clean beauty, creating content that highlights the shared commitment to natural products.

Fostering Genuine Relationships

Building authentic partnerships requires more than just a transactional approach. Foster genuine relationships by engaging with influencers' content and showing genuine interest in their work. Comment on their posts, share their content, and establish a rapport before proposing a collaboration.

When you approach influencers, personalize your communication. Highlight why you believe they are a great fit for your brand and how you envision the partnership. Authenticity in your outreach sets the tone for a genuine relationship. For example, rather than sending a generic message, mention specific posts or campaigns of theirs that you admire and explain how your brand aligns with their content.

Co-Creating Content

Authentic partnerships thrive on co-created content that reflects the influencer's voice and style while integrating your brand seamlessly. Allow influencers creative freedom to develop content that resonates with their audience. This approach ensures that the content feels natural and authentic, rather than forced or scripted.

Work collaboratively with influencers to brainstorm ideas and develop a content plan. Provide them with key messages and product details, but trust their expertise in creating engaging content. For instance, a fashion brand might send a new collection to an influencer and collaborate on a styled photoshoot or fashion haul video that showcases the pieces in a way that feels organic and true to the influencer's style.

Transparency and Trust

Transparency is crucial in building trust with influencers and their audiences. Be clear about your expectations, deliverables, and compensation from the start. Ensure that influencers disclose their partnerships with your brand in compliance with advertising guidelines.

Trust is a two-way street. Trust influencers to know their audience and create content that will resonate. Avoid micromanaging the process, as this can stifle creativity and authenticity. A successful partnership is one where both parties feel valued and respected. For example, if you are collaborating on a product review, allow the influencer to share their honest opinions and experiences, even if it includes constructive feedback.

Measuring Success and Providing Feedback

After launching a campaign, it's important to measure its success and provide feedback. Analyze key metrics such as engagement rates, reach, and conversions to assess the impact of the partnership. Share these insights with the influencer, celebrating successes and discussing areas for improvement.

Regularly review the performance of your collaborations and seek feedback from influencers about their experience working with your brand. This continuous improvement process strengthens the partnership and paves the way for future collaborations. For instance, after a successful campaign, a food brand might debrief with the influencer to discuss what worked well and brainstorm ideas for upcoming projects.

Building authentic partnerships with influencers is a strategic and thoughtful process. By identifying the right influencers, establishing mutual goals, fostering genuine relationships, co-creating content, maintaining transparency, and measuring success, you can create collaborations that are both impactful and enduring. These authentic partnerships not only enhance your brand's presence on social media but also build lasting connections with influencers and their audiences.

Measuring Influencer Impact

Before measuring the impact of your influencer marketing efforts, it's essential to set clear and specific objectives. What do you hope to achieve through these campaigns? Objectives might include increasing brand awareness, boosting sales, driving website traffic, or enhancing engagement rates. Defining these goals upfront provides a framework for evaluating success and guiding your measurement strategy.

Tracking Engagement Metrics

Engagement metrics are a vital indicator of an influencer's impact. These metrics include likes, comments, shares, and saves on posts. High engagement levels suggest that the content resonates with the audience and encourages interaction.

To assess these metrics, you can use tools like Social Blade, Hootsuite, or Sprout Social, which provide detailed analytics on social media interactions. Comparing engagement rates before, during, and after your campaign can help determine the influencer's effectiveness in engaging their audience with your brand.

Monitoring Traffic and Conversions

One of the most direct ways to measure influencer impact is by tracking the traffic and conversions generated from their posts. Utilize unique tracking links or UTM parameters to monitor how much traffic an influencer drives to your website. Google Analytics is an excellent tool for this, allowing you to see not only the volume of traffic but also the behavior of visitors once they arrive.

Additionally, tracking conversion rates is crucial. Whether your goal is to increase sales, sign-ups, or downloads, understanding how many of the influencer-driven visitors complete these actions will provide clear insights into the campaign's effectiveness.

Analyzing Reach and Impressions

Reach and impressions are fundamental metrics for understanding how many people saw your influencer's content. Reach refers to the total number of unique users who viewed the content, while impressions indicate how many times the content was viewed in total.

Tools like Instagram Insights, Facebook Analytics, and X Analytics offer data on reach and impressions, helping you gauge the overall visibility of your campaign. These metrics are particularly important for brand awareness objectives, indicating the breadth of your campaign's exposure.

Evaluating Content Performance

Beyond quantitative metrics, qualitative analysis of content performance is also essential. Review the comments and feedback on the influencer's posts to gauge audience sentiment. Are followers positively engaging with the content? Are they expressing interest in your brand or products?

User-generated content can also be a valuable indicator. If the influencer's followers are creating their own posts about your brand, it demonstrates a high level of engagement and enthusiasm. Monitoring hashtags and mentions related to your campaign can provide deeper insights into how the content is being received and shared.

Measuring ROI

Calculating the return on investment (ROI) is critical for understanding the financial impact of your influencer campaigns. To calculate ROI, compare the revenue generated from the campaign against the costs involved, including influencer fees, production costs, and any additional expenses.

ROI = (Revenue from Campaign - Campaign Costs) / Campaign Costs

A positive ROI indicates that the campaign was profitable, while a negative ROI suggests that it did not generate enough revenue to cover the costs. Regularly measuring ROI helps you refine your strategies and allocate your budget more effectively in future campaigns.

Using Surveys and Feedback

Direct feedback from your audience can provide valuable insights into the impact of your influencer campaigns. Conducting surveys or polls can help you understand how your audience perceives the influencer collaboration and whether it influenced their purchasing decisions or brand perception.

Incorporating feedback mechanisms into your campaigns allows you to gather firsthand data on audience reactions and preferences. This qualitative data complements the quantitative metrics, offering a more comprehensive view of your campaign's effectiveness.

Continuous Improvement

Influencer marketing is not a one-time effort but an ongoing process. Continuously analyzing and learning from each campaign is essential for long-term success. Regularly review your metrics, experiment with different types of content and influencers, and adapt your strategies based on what you learn.

By maintaining a cycle of measurement, analysis, and improvement, you can enhance the impact of your influencer marketing efforts, ensuring that each campaign builds on the successes and lessons of the previous ones.

Measuring the impact of influencer marketing requires a combination of quantitative metrics and qualitative insights. By setting clear objectives, tracking key metrics, and continuously refining your approach, you can maximize the effectiveness of your influencer partnerships and achieve your marketing goals.

Navigating Challenges

In the ever-evolving landscape of social media marketing, challenges are inevitable. Whether it's adapting to algorithm changes, handling negative feedback, or keeping up with emerging trends, marketers must be prepared to navigate these obstacles effectively. Understanding and addressing these challenges head-on can turn potential setbacks into opportunities for growth and innovation. Here are some common challenges and strategies for overcoming them.

Adapting to Algorithm Changes

One of the most frequent challenges in social media marketing is adapting to the constant changes in platform algorithms. These changes can significantly impact your content's visibility and engagement rates. To stay ahead, it's crucial to keep informed about updates and adjust your strategies accordingly.

Firstly, diversify your content and experiment with different formats. If an algorithm prioritizes video content, consider incorporating more videos into your posts. Engaging with your audience through comments, likes, and shares can also boost your content's visibility, as platforms often reward active engagement.

Another strategy is to analyze performance metrics regularly. Identify what types of content are performing well and which are not, then adjust your approach based on these insights. For example, if Instagram's algorithm favors Stories over static posts, increase your use of Stories to maintain and grow your reach.

Managing Negative Feedback

Negative feedback is a reality for any brand with an online presence. How you handle criticism can significantly affect your brand's reputation. The key is to respond promptly and constructively, showing that you value customer feedback and are committed to improvement.

When addressing negative comments, maintain a professional and empathetic tone. Acknowledge the issue, apologize if necessary, and provide a solution. For instance, if a customer complains about a product defect, offer a replacement or a refund. This not only resolves the immediate problem but also demonstrates your commitment to customer satisfaction.

In cases of widespread criticism or a social media crisis, transparency is vital. Communicate openly about the steps you are taking to address the issue. This approach can help rebuild trust and show that you take your customers' concerns seriously.

Keeping Up with Trends

The fast-paced nature of social media means that trends come and go rapidly. Staying relevant requires continuous monitoring and adaptation. Use social media listening tools to track emerging trends and conversations within your industry. These tools can help you identify new opportunities to engage with your audience and keep your content fresh and relevant.

Participate in trending conversations when they align with your brand values and message. For example, if there is a trending hashtag related to sustainability and your brand promotes eco-friendly products, join the conversation with relevant content. However, avoid jumping on trends that don't align with your brand, as this can come across as inauthentic.

Ensuring Consistent Engagement

Maintaining consistent engagement with your audience can be challenging, especially as your follower base grows. Consistency in posting and interacting with your audience is crucial to keep them engaged and loyal. Develop a content calendar to plan your posts in advance, ensuring a regular flow of content.

Automate routine tasks such as scheduling posts and monitoring engagement using social media management tools. This allows you to focus more on creating quality content and engaging with your audience. However, balance automation with personal interaction. Respond to comments and messages personally to build a stronger connection with your audience.

Balancing Quantity and Quality

Another challenge is finding the right balance between the quantity and quality of content. While it's important to post regularly, the quality of your content should never be compromised. Posting too frequently with low-quality content can lead to audience fatigue and decreased engagement.

Prioritize creating high-quality content that provides value to your audience. This could be informative articles, entertaining videos, or visually appealing images. It's better to post less frequently but with higher quality than to flood your feed with mediocre content.

Measuring Success

Finally, accurately measuring the success of your social media efforts can be complex. It's essential to define clear metrics that align with your goals, whether it's brand awareness, engagement, or conversions. Use analytics tools to track these metrics and gain insights into your performance.

Regularly review and analyze your data to understand what's working and what's not. Adjust your strategies based on these insights to continuously improve your results. For example, if you notice that posts with user-generated content receive higher engagement, incorporate more of this type of content into your strategy.

Navigating the challenges of social media marketing requires flexibility, strategic thinking, and a proactive approach. By staying informed, engaging authentically with your audience, and continuously adapting your strategies, you can turn potential obstacles into opportunities for growth and success.

Chapter 5: Engaging Your Audience

Building Community

Building a strong community around your brand is one of the most powerful strategies for long-term success. A loyal community doesn't just buy your products; they advocate for your brand, provide valuable feedback, and create a sense of belonging that goes beyond mere transactions. In today's digital age, fostering a vibrant, engaged community can set your brand apart and drive sustained growth.

Creating a Sense of Belonging

To build a community, start by creating a sense of belonging. Your audience should feel like they are part of something special. This begins with understanding their values, interests, and pain points. Engage with them on a personal level, and show genuine interest in their experiences and opinions.

One effective way to foster belonging is through storytelling. Share your brand's journey, mission, and values in a way that resonates with your audience. Highlight customer stories and testimonials to show that you value their contributions. When people see themselves reflected in your brand's narrative, they are more likely to develop a strong connection and loyalty.

Encouraging Interaction and Engagement

Active engagement is the lifeblood of any community. Encourage interaction by creating content that invites participation. Ask questions, solicit opinions, and create opportunities for your audience to share their own content. User-generated content not only boosts engagement but also strengthens the community by highlighting diverse voices within it.

Social media platforms offer various tools to facilitate interaction. Use live streams to host Q&A sessions, webinars, or behind-the-scenes tours. Create polls, quizzes, and challenges that encourage your audience to get involved. These activities not only keep your community engaged but also provide valuable insights into their preferences and behaviors.

Providing Value

Communities thrive when they feel they are receiving value. Provide content and experiences that are beneficial to your audience. This could be in the form of educational content, exclusive offers, or early access to new products. The key is to consistently deliver something that enhances their lives or solves their problems.

Consider creating a content calendar that includes a mix of informative, entertaining, and exclusive content. Educational posts can position your brand as an authority in your industry, while entertaining content can build emotional connections. Exclusive offers and early access perks can make your community members feel valued and appreciated.

Fostering Inclusivity and Respect

An inclusive and respectful environment is essential for a healthy community. Ensure that your community guidelines promote positivity and respect for all members. Address negative behavior promptly and fairly to maintain a safe space for everyone.

Inclusivity means recognizing and celebrating diversity within your community. Highlight different voices and perspectives, and ensure that everyone feels welcome and valued. This approach not only strengthens the community but also enriches it with a wide range of experiences and insights.

Building Relationships with Community Leaders

Identify and nurture relationships with key members of your community who have the potential to influence others. These community leaders can be brand ambassadors, moderators, or simply highly engaged members. Their active participation can help drive engagement and set the tone for the rest of the community.

Work closely with these leaders to understand their needs and perspectives. Provide them with the tools and support they need to succeed in their roles. Recognizing and rewarding their contributions can further motivate them and solidify their loyalty to your brand.

Measuring Community Health

Regularly assess the health of your community to ensure it continues to thrive. Look beyond vanity metrics like follower count and focus on meaningful engagement indicators. Monitor metrics such as active participation, repeat interactions, and sentiment analysis to gauge the overall health and happiness of your community.

Use surveys and feedback forms to gather direct input from your community members. This can provide valuable insights into what they value and where there may be opportunities for improvement. By actively listening and responding to their needs, you can ensure your community remains vibrant and engaged.

Adapting and Growing

Communities are dynamic and evolve over time. Stay flexible and be willing to adapt your strategies based on feedback and changing circumstances. Regularly introduce new initiatives to keep things fresh and exciting for your members.

Embrace innovation and stay ahead of trends that may impact your community. Whether it's new social media features, emerging platforms, or shifts in audience behavior, staying informed and adaptable will help you maintain a strong, engaged community.

Building a community is an ongoing process that requires dedication, empathy, and creativity. By creating a sense of belonging, encouraging interaction, providing value, fostering inclusivity, and staying adaptable, you can cultivate a loyal and vibrant community that supports your brand's growth and success.

Interactive Content

Interactive content stands out as a powerful tool for engaging audiences. Unlike static posts, interactive content invites users to participate, creating a more dynamic and immersive experience. This not only captures attention but also fosters a deeper connection between the brand and its audience. Here's how to harness the power of interactive content to enhance your social media strategy.

The Appeal of Interactive Content

Interactive content is inherently engaging because it transforms passive consumption into active participation. Users are more likely to remember and share content they've engaged with personally. This type of content can take many forms, from polls and quizzes to live videos and interactive stories. Each format offers unique ways to capture audience interest and encourage them to interact with your brand.

For instance, a beauty brand might create a quiz that helps users determine their ideal skincare routine based on their skin type and concerns. This not only provides valuable information but also drives engagement by encouraging users to participate and share their results.

Polls and Quizzes

Polls and quizzes are among the most popular forms of interactive content on social media. They are easy to create and can provide immediate feedback and insights from your audience. Polls can be used to gauge opinions, preferences, or even for market research. Quizzes, on the other hand, can entertain and educate, making them highly shareable.

For example, a fitness brand could run a poll asking followers about their favorite types of workouts. The results can inform future content while also sparking discussions among followers. A quiz titled "What's Your Fitness Personality?" can engage users and encourage them to share their results, expanding the brand's reach.

Live Videos

Live videos offer real-time interaction, making them incredibly engaging. They provide a sense of immediacy and authenticity, allowing brands to connect with their audience on a personal level. Live videos can be used for various purposes, such as product launches, Q&A sessions, behind-the-scenes looks, and live tutorials.

A tech company might host a live Q&A session to answer questions about a new product. This not only builds excitement but also allows the brand to address concerns and highlight features in real time. The interactive nature of live videos encourages viewers to participate by asking questions and sharing their thoughts.

Interactive Stories

Platforms like Instagram and Facebook have introduced features that make stories a powerful tool for interaction. Stickers, polls, questions, and swipe-up links can be incorporated into stories to engage viewers. These features make stories not just a way to share updates, but a means to foster direct interaction with your audience.

For instance, a travel agency could use Instagram Stories to showcase different destinations and include polls asking followers to vote on their preferred travel spots. This engagement can provide valuable insights while also making followers feel involved in the content creation process.

Contests and Giveaways

Contests and giveaways are effective ways to boost engagement and grow your audience. They encourage users to interact with your content by offering them something in return, such as a prize. To participate, users might be asked to like, comment, share, or create their own content related to your brand.

A fashion brand could host a photo contest where followers share their best outfit styled with the brand's clothing. Not only does this generate a wealth of user-generated content, but it also increases visibility and engagement as participants share their entries with their networks.

Interactive Infographics and Videos

Interactive infographics and videos can transform complex information into engaging and digestible content. These formats allow users to click, explore, and discover information at their own pace. Interactive elements like clickable charts, embedded videos, and animation can make data and stories more compelling.

A health organization might create an interactive infographic about healthy eating habits, where users can click on different food groups to learn more about their benefits. This engaging format helps to educate while keeping the audience interested.

Interactive content is a powerful way to capture and maintain audience interest on social media. By incorporating polls, quizzes, live videos, interactive stories, contests, and interactive infographics, you can create a dynamic and engaging social media presence. This approach not only enhances user experience but also fosters a deeper connection with your audience, driving higher engagement and loyalty.

Responding to Feedback

Feedback from your audience is an invaluable resource for improving your products, services, and overall brand experience. It provides direct insights into customer satisfaction, areas for improvement, and potential innovations. Responding to feedback effectively can transform casual customers into loyal advocates and can help you build a stronger, more responsive brand.

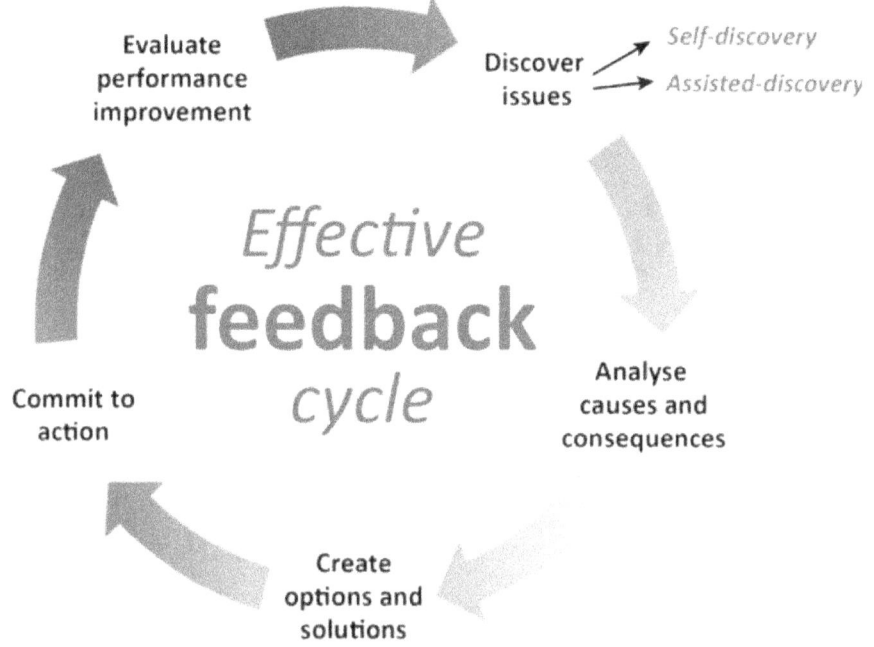

The Effective Feedback Cycle in Social Media Engagement. Source: hyperisland.com

Listening Actively

Active listening is the foundation of responding to feedback. This involves not just hearing what your audience says, but truly understanding their perspectives and emotions. Pay attention to the details in their comments, reviews, and messages. Recognize recurring themes and specific pain points they mention.

Active listening can be facilitated through various channels. Monitor your social media platforms, review sites, and direct customer communications regularly. Use tools like social listening software to track mentions of your brand and keywords related to your products. This comprehensive approach ensures you don't miss important feedback and can respond promptly.

Acknowledging and Appreciating

When someone takes the time to provide feedback, acknowledge their effort and show appreciation. This simple act can go a long way in building a positive relationship with your audience. Even if the feedback is negative, thanking the person for their input demonstrates that you value their opinion and are committed to improving.

Personalize your responses where possible. Use the customer's name and reference specific points they made in their feedback. This level of personalization shows that you are genuinely engaged and not just offering a generic reply.

Addressing Concerns Transparently

When responding to negative feedback, transparency is key. Address the concerns directly and honestly. If a mistake was made, acknowledge it and explain the steps you are taking to rectify the issue. Offering a sincere apology and a clear plan of action can help rebuild trust and show your commitment to customer satisfaction.

For instance, if a customer complains about a product defect, you might respond by explaining the issue, detailing how you plan to fix it, and offering a replacement or refund. Transparency not only resolves the immediate concern but also sets a precedent for how your brand handles challenges.

Turning Feedback into Action

Listening and acknowledging feedback is only the beginning. The real impact comes from turning that feedback into actionable improvements. Regularly analyze the feedback you receive to identify common themes and areas where changes are needed.

Develop a system for tracking feedback and the corresponding actions taken. Share updates with your audience to show that their feedback leads to tangible changes. For example, if multiple customers suggest a new feature for your app, update them when the feature is in development and again when it's launched. This continuous loop of feedback and action fosters a collaborative relationship with your audience.

Engaging in Meaningful Dialogue

Feedback offers an opportunity for dialogue, not just a one-off response. Engage with your audience in meaningful conversations to deepen their connection with your brand. Ask follow-up questions to gain more insights, and invite them to participate in beta tests or surveys for upcoming products.

For example, if a customer praises your customer service, you might ask what specific aspects they appreciated and how you can further improve. This approach not only provides more detailed feedback but also makes customers feel valued and involved in your brand's development.

Leveraging Positive Feedback

Positive feedback is a powerful tool for building your brand's reputation. Share testimonials, success stories, and customer reviews on your website and social media channels. Highlighting positive experiences reinforces your brand's value and can influence potential customers.

When sharing positive feedback, always seek permission from the customer and give them credit. This not only respects their privacy but also enhances authenticity. Highlighting real customer stories can create a more relatable and trustworthy image for your brand.

Building a Culture of Feedback

Encourage a culture of feedback within your organization. Train your team to value and respond to feedback constructively. Foster an environment where feedback is seen as an opportunity for growth rather than criticism.

Regularly update your team on feedback trends and the actions being taken in response. This ensures everyone is aligned and committed to continuous improvement. A culture that values feedback at all levels can lead to more innovative solutions and a more responsive brand.

Responding to feedback effectively is an ongoing process that requires active listening, transparency, action, and engagement. By valuing and acting on feedback, you can build stronger relationships with your audience, drive continuous improvement, and ultimately create a more loyal and satisfied customer base.

Managing Negative Feedback

Handling negative feedback on social media is a crucial aspect of maintaining a positive brand image. Negative comments or reviews can seem daunting, but they also provide valuable opportunities to demonstrate your commitment to customer satisfaction and improvement. Here's how to manage negative feedback effectively and turn potential setbacks into positive outcomes.

Respond Promptly and Professionally

One of the most important steps in managing negative feedback is to respond quickly. A prompt response shows that you are attentive and care about your customers' concerns. Delays can make the issue seem unimportant to your brand and may escalate the situation.

When crafting your response, maintain a professional and courteous tone. Acknowledge the customer's feelings and apologize for any inconvenience they may have experienced. Even if you believe the criticism is unfounded, it's important to show empathy and understanding. For example, "We're sorry to hear about your experience and appreciate your feedback."

Address the Issue Directly

After acknowledging the feedback, address the specific issue raised by the customer. Provide a clear explanation or solution to the problem. If the issue requires further investigation or details that are not appropriate for a public forum, invite the customer to continue the conversation privately through direct messages or email.

For instance, if a customer complains about a delayed delivery, you could respond: "We apologize for the delay in your order. Please send us a direct message with your order number so we can resolve this for you as quickly as possible."

Take the Conversation Offline

For more complex or sensitive issues, it's often best to move the conversation offline. This allows for a more detailed discussion and resolution without the scrutiny of the public eye. Offer a direct line of communication such as a customer service email or phone number where the issue can be handled more privately and effectively.

For example, "We're sorry for the inconvenience. Could you please contact our customer service team at [email/phone] so we can assist you further?"

Learn from Feedback

Negative feedback can provide valuable insights into areas where your business can improve. Analyze recurring issues or complaints to identify potential weaknesses in your products, services, or customer experience. Use this information to make necessary changes and enhancements.

Share feedback with relevant departments and involve your team in developing solutions. For example, if multiple customers are experiencing issues with a particular product, collaborate with your product development team to investigate and address the problem.

Show Transparency

Transparency is key in managing negative feedback effectively. If your brand has made a mistake, openly acknowledge it and explain the steps you are taking to rectify the situation. This honesty can build trust with your audience and demonstrate your commitment to improvement.

For example, if a technical glitch has affected multiple customers, a public post acknowledging the issue and providing updates on the resolution process can reassure your audience that you are actively working on a solution.

Highlight Positive Outcomes

Once an issue has been resolved, consider sharing the positive outcome publicly. This can show that your brand takes customer feedback seriously and is dedicated to resolving problems. Always ensure that you have the customer's permission to share their experience.

For instance, a follow-up post saying, "We're happy to report that the issue affecting our delivery times has been resolved. Thank you to our customers for your patience and feedback," can highlight your responsiveness and commitment to service.

Maintain Consistency

Consistency in your responses is crucial. Ensure that all team members handling social media interactions are trained to manage negative feedback in a professional and empathetic manner. Develop guidelines and protocols for addressing common issues to maintain a unified brand voice.

For example, create a response template that team members can customize for different situations, ensuring that all communications reflect your brand's values and commitment to customer satisfaction.

Managing negative feedback effectively can enhance your brand's reputation and build stronger relationships with your customers. By responding promptly and professionally, addressing issues directly, taking conversations offline when necessary, learning from feedback, showing transparency, highlighting positive outcomes, and maintaining consistency, you can turn negative experiences into opportunities for improvement and trust-building.

Chapter 6: Data-Driven Social Media Marketing

Understanding Social Media Analytics

Social media analytics provides the insights necessary to understand your audience, evaluate the effectiveness of your strategies, and refine your approach for better results. Without analytics, your efforts are akin to navigating in the dark—possible but far from optimal.

Key Metrics to Track

Understanding social media analytics starts with knowing which metrics matter. While the specific metrics can vary depending on your goals, several key performance indicators (KPIs) are universally important.

Engagement Metrics: These include likes, comments, shares, and saves. Engagement metrics tell you how well your content resonates with your audience. High engagement indicates that your content is interesting and relevant to your followers.

Reach and Impressions: Reach refers to the number of unique users who have seen your content, while impressions count the total number of times your content has been displayed. These metrics help gauge the visibility of your content.

Follower Growth: Tracking the increase or decrease in your follower count over time can provide insights into the overall health of your social media presence. A steady growth in followers usually indicates a successful strategy.

Click-Through Rate (CTR): This metric measures how often people click on the links in your posts. A high CTR indicates that your content is compelling enough to drive traffic to your website or other destinations.

Conversion Rate: Ultimately, you want your social media efforts to lead to conversions, whether they are sales, sign-ups, or downloads. Conversion rate measures the percentage of users who take a desired action after interacting with your content.

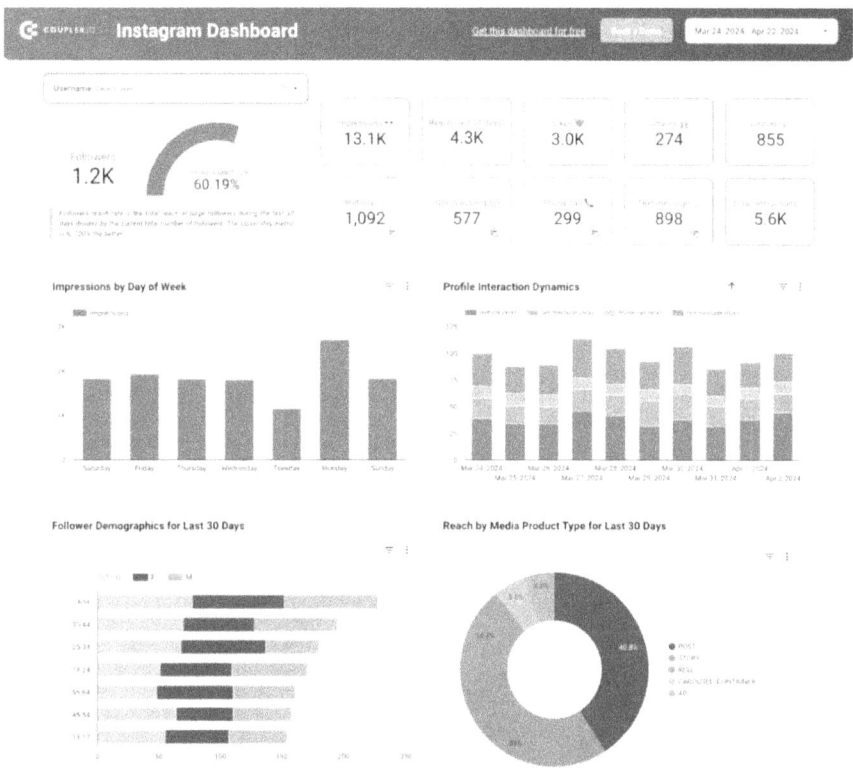

Instagram Analytics Dashboard Example. Source: coupler.io

Tools for Social Media Analytics

Several tools can help you gather and analyze social media data. These tools range from platform-specific analytics to comprehensive third-party solutions.

Platform Analytics: Most social media platforms offer built-in analytics tools. Facebook Insights, X Analytics, Instagram Insights, and LinkedIn Analytics provide a wealth of data specific to each platform. These tools are a great starting point for understanding your performance.

Google Analytics: For a more holistic view, Google Analytics can track social media traffic to your website, providing insights into user behavior once they leave the social platform.

Third-Party Tools: Tools like Hootsuite, Sprout Social, and Buffer offer advanced analytics and reporting features. They can aggregate data from multiple platforms, making it easier to get a comprehensive view of your social media performance.

Interpreting Data for Actionable Insights

Collecting data is only the first step; the real value lies in interpreting it to gain actionable insights. Look for patterns and trends that can inform your strategy.

For example, if you notice that posts with videos consistently receive higher engagement, consider incorporating more video content into your strategy. If your follower growth has plateaued, analyze the content and posting times to identify potential improvements.

Context is crucial. Compare your metrics against industry benchmarks and your own historical performance to gauge success. A spike in engagement during a campaign period might indicate that your strategy is working, while a sudden drop could signal the need for adjustment.

The Role of Sentiment Analysis

Beyond quantitative metrics, sentiment analysis helps you understand the qualitative aspect of social media interactions. Sentiment analysis tools assess the tone of comments and mentions, categorizing them as positive, negative, or neutral.

This analysis can reveal how your audience feels about your brand, products, or specific campaigns. Monitoring sentiment over time helps you identify potential issues early and address them before they escalate.

Continuous Improvement

Social media analytics is not a one-time task but an ongoing process. Regularly review your metrics to understand what's working and what's not. Use these insights to experiment with different types of content, posting times, and engagement strategies.

Set specific, measurable goals for your social media efforts and use analytics to track your progress. This iterative process of analyzing data, refining strategies, and measuring outcomes is key to optimizing your social media presence and achieving your business objectives.

Understanding social media analytics empowers you to make data-driven decisions that enhance your marketing efforts. By focusing on the right metrics, using the best tools, and interpreting data for actionable insights, you can build a robust and effective social media strategy that drives meaningful results.

Tools for Data Analysis

Data analysis is crucial for making informed decisions and optimizing your strategy. The right tools can provide insights into your audience, measure campaign performance, and identify trends. Here are some essential tools for data analysis that can help you turn raw data into actionable insights.

Google Analytics

Google Analytics is a powerful tool for tracking and analyzing website traffic. It provides detailed insights into how users interact with your site, where they come from, and what content they engage with the most. By linking Google Analytics with your social media accounts, you can track the effectiveness of your social media campaigns in driving traffic and conversions.

For instance, Google Analytics can show you which social media platforms generate the most traffic to your website, allowing you to allocate resources more effectively. You can also track specific goals, such as newsletter sign-ups or product purchases, to measure the ROI of your social media efforts.

Hootsuite Analytics

Hootsuite is a comprehensive social media management tool that includes robust analytics features. It allows you to track the performance of your posts across multiple platforms in one place. Hootsuite Analytics provides metrics such as engagement, reach, and clicks, helping you understand which content resonates with your audience.

The tool also offers customizable reports, enabling you to focus on the metrics that matter most to your business. For example, you can create a report that highlights your top-performing posts, the best times to post, and the demographics of your audience. This information can guide your content strategy and improve your social media performance.

Sprout Social

Sprout Social is another versatile tool that combines social media management with powerful analytics. It provides detailed reports on audience demographics, engagement, and content performance. Sprout Social's listening tool can track brand mentions and sentiment, giving you insights into how your brand is perceived online.

With Sprout Social, you can also benchmark your performance against competitors. This feature helps you understand your position in the market and identify areas for improvement. For example, if a competitor's posts are receiving higher engagement, you can analyze their content strategy and adjust yours accordingly.

Socialbakers

Socialbakers offers a range of analytics tools designed to help brands understand their social media performance. It provides insights into audience demographics, content effectiveness, and competitive analysis. Socialbakers' AI-powered tools can predict trends and suggest optimal posting times, helping you stay ahead of the curve.

The platform's content intelligence feature analyzes the performance of different content types, such as videos, images, and text posts. This allows you to identify what kind of content your audience prefers and tailor your strategy accordingly. For example, if video content consistently outperforms other types, you might decide to invest more in video production.

Buffer Analyze

Buffer Analyze is a user-friendly tool that provides clear and concise insights into your social media performance. It tracks key metrics such as engagement, reach, and follower growth across various platforms. Buffer's simple interface makes it easy to understand your data and identify trends.

One of Buffer's standout features is its recommendations for improving your social media strategy. Based on your data, Buffer can suggest the best times to post, which hashtags to use, and what types of content to focus on. This actionable advice can help you enhance your social media presence and achieve better results.

Keyhole

Keyhole is a real-time social media analytics and reporting tool that tracks hashtags, keywords, and accounts. It provides detailed insights into your campaigns, including reach, engagement, and sentiment analysis. Keyhole's tracking capabilities are especially useful for monitoring the impact of specific marketing campaigns or events.

For example, if you're running a campaign with a unique hashtag, Keyhole can show you how many times the hashtag has been used, the reach of those posts, and the overall sentiment. This information helps you gauge the success of your campaign and make data-driven adjustments.

Tableau

Tableau is a data visualization tool that can transform complex data sets into interactive and easy-to-understand visualizations. While not specific to social media, Tableau can be integrated with various social media analytics tools to create comprehensive dashboards that provide a holistic view of your social media performance.

With Tableau, you can create custom visualizations that highlight key metrics, trends, and correlations. For instance, you can visualize the relationship between posting frequency and engagement rates, helping you optimize your content calendar. Tableau's powerful analytics capabilities make it an invaluable tool for data-driven marketers.

Using these tools for data analysis allows you to gain deep insights into your social media performance, understand your audience better, and make informed decisions. By leveraging the strengths of each tool, you can develop a comprehensive and effective social media strategy that drives engagement, growth, and success.

Making Data-Driven Decisions

Making data-driven decisions involves leveraging quantitative and qualitative data to guide your strategy, optimize your campaigns, and achieve better outcomes. This approach ensures that your decisions are grounded in reality and tailored to meet the needs of your audience.

Setting Clear Objectives and KPIs

The first step in making data-driven decisions is setting clear objectives and key performance indicators (KPIs). What do you want to achieve with your social media efforts? Whether it's increasing brand awareness, boosting engagement, driving website traffic, or generating leads, having well-defined goals allows you to measure success accurately.

KPIs should be specific, measurable, achievable, relevant, and time-bound (SMART). For example, instead of setting a vague goal like "increase engagement," aim for "boost Instagram engagement by 20% over the next three months." Clear objectives and KPIs provide a focused direction and a basis for measuring your progress.

Collecting and Analyzing Relevant Data

Once your goals are set, the next step is to collect and analyze relevant data. Utilize social media analytics tools to gather insights on your performance. Platforms like Facebook Insights, X Analytics, and Instagram Insights offer detailed metrics on reach, engagement, and audience demographics.

Analyze this data to identify patterns and trends. Look for correlations between your content strategies and performance metrics. For example, if you notice that posts with behind-the-scenes content consistently generate higher engagement, this insight can inform your future content planning.

Turning Insights into Actionable Strategies

Data analysis should lead to actionable insights. Rather than getting bogged down by numbers, focus on what the data tells you about your audience's preferences and behaviors. Use these insights to refine your content strategy, posting schedule, and overall approach.

For instance, if data shows that your audience is most active in the evenings, adjust your posting schedule to align with these peak times. If certain types of posts—such as user-generated content or educational videos—perform better, incorporate more of these into your content mix.

Experimentation and A/B Testing

Experimentation is a key component of data-driven decision making. A/B testing, or split testing, involves comparing two versions of a piece of content or an ad to see which performs better. This method allows you to test variables such as headlines, images, calls to action, and posting times.

Conducting A/B tests helps you understand what resonates most with your audience. For example, you might test two different headlines for a Facebook ad campaign to determine which one drives more clicks. Use the results to optimize your campaigns, ensuring that your efforts are continually improving.

Monitoring and Adjusting in Real Time

Social media is dynamic, and your strategy should be too. Regularly monitor your performance metrics to stay informed about how your content and campaigns are performing. Real-time data allows you to make quick adjustments and respond to emerging trends.

If you notice a sudden drop in engagement, investigate the possible causes and make necessary changes. Conversely, if a particular post goes viral, analyze what made it successful and try to replicate those elements in future content.

Leveraging Predictive Analytics

Predictive analytics takes data-driven decision making to the next level. By analyzing historical data and identifying patterns, predictive analytics can forecast future trends and behaviors. This insight helps you anticipate your audience's needs and stay ahead of the competition.

For example, if predictive analytics indicates a growing interest in a specific topic within your industry, you can create content around that topic to capture your audience's attention. This proactive approach ensures that your strategy remains relevant and impactful.

Building a Culture of Data-Driven Decisions

Finally, fostering a culture of data-driven decision making within your organization is crucial. Encourage your team to rely on data and insights rather than assumptions. Provide training on analytics tools and emphasize the importance of continuous learning and adaptation.

Regularly share data insights and performance reports with your team. Celebrate successes that result from data-driven strategies and analyze failures to learn and improve. This culture of data-driven decision making promotes accountability, innovation, and sustained growth.

Making data-driven decisions transforms your social media strategy from guesswork to precision. By setting clear objectives, collecting and analyzing relevant data, turning insights into action, experimenting, monitoring, leveraging predictive analytics, and fostering a data-driven culture, you can optimize your efforts and achieve greater success in your social media marketing endeavors.

Predictive Analytics

Predictive analytics offers a revolutionary approach to understanding and anticipating customer behavior. By leveraging data, algorithms, and machine learning, predictive analytics can forecast future trends, enabling marketers to make proactive and informed decisions. This forward-looking perspective can transform your strategy from reactive to strategic, giving you a competitive edge.

Understanding Predictive Analytics

Predictive analytics involves using historical data to predict future outcomes. It combines statistical techniques, machine learning, and data mining to analyze current and historical facts, making predictions about future events. In marketing, this means anticipating user behavior, engagement patterns, and market trends based on past data.

For instance, by analyzing past engagement metrics, such as likes, shares, and comments, predictive analytics can forecast which types of content are likely to perform well in the future. This allows you to tailor your content approach to maximize engagement and reach.

Enhancing Content Strategy

One of the most significant benefits of predictive analytics is its ability to enhance your content planning. By understanding which types of content have historically performed well, you can predict future success and optimize your content accordingly. This involves analyzing variables such as post type, timing, and audience demographics.

For example, if your data shows that video posts receive higher engagement on weekends, you can prioritize creating and scheduling video content for those days. Similarly, predictive analytics can help identify the best times to post for maximum visibility, ensuring your content reaches the largest possible audience when they are most active.

Personalizing User Experience

Predictive analytics also plays a crucial role in personalizing the user experience. By analyzing user behavior and preferences, you can deliver more relevant and personalized content. This not only enhances user satisfaction but also increases the likelihood of engagement and conversion.

For instance, e-commerce brands can use predictive analytics to recommend products based on past purchases and browsing history. Social media platforms can suggest content tailored to individual user interests, increasing the chances of interaction. This level of personalization fosters a deeper connection with your audience, encouraging loyalty and repeat engagement.

Improving Ad Targeting

Effective ad targeting is essential for maximizing return on investment (ROI) in social media advertising. Predictive analytics can significantly improve ad targeting by identifying potential customers who are most likely to convert. By analyzing past behaviors, such as website visits, purchase history, and engagement with previous ads, predictive models can pinpoint high-value audiences.

For example, a predictive model might reveal that users who frequently engage with product tutorials are more likely to make a purchase. With this insight, you can target similar users with ads featuring tutorials, increasing the chances of conversion. This targeted approach ensures your ad spend is directed toward the most promising prospects, enhancing overall campaign efficiency.

Anticipating Market Trends

Staying ahead of market trends is crucial for maintaining a competitive edge. Predictive analytics enables you to anticipate shifts in market dynamics, allowing you to adapt your strategy proactively. By analyzing industry data and social media conversations, predictive models can identify emerging trends and potential opportunities.

For example, if predictive analytics indicates a growing interest in sustainable products, a fashion brand can start promoting its eco-friendly line before the trend becomes mainstream. This proactive approach not only positions the brand as a leader but also captures early adopters, driving early engagement and sales.

Mitigating Risks

Predictive analytics can also help mitigate risks by identifying potential issues before they escalate. By monitoring social media sentiment and engagement patterns, predictive models can alert you to negative trends, such as declining engagement or increasing negative feedback.

For instance, if predictive analytics detects a rise in negative comments about a recent product launch, you can investigate and address the underlying issues promptly. This allows you to take corrective action, such as improving the product or clarifying misconceptions, before the situation worsens. Proactively managing potential risks protects your brand's reputation and maintains customer trust.

Optimizing Resource Allocation

Efficient resource allocation is essential for maximizing the impact of your social media efforts. Predictive analytics can guide resource allocation by identifying high-performing strategies and channels. By understanding which activities generate the best results, you can allocate your time, budget, and efforts more effectively.

For example, if data shows that influencer partnerships drive significant engagement and conversions, you can invest more in these collaborations. Conversely, if certain social media channels yield low returns, you can reallocate resources to more productive areas. This data-driven approach ensures that your resources are used optimally, maximizing overall efficiency and effectiveness.

Predictive analytics offers a powerful tool for transforming your social media marketing strategy. By forecasting future trends, personalizing user experiences, improving ad targeting, anticipating market shifts, mitigating risks, and optimizing resource allocation, predictive analytics enables you to make proactive and informed decisions. Embracing this technology can give you a significant competitive advantage, positioning your brand for sustained success in the dynamic world of social media.

Chapter 7: Paid Advertising Strategies

Introduction to Social Media Ads

Social media ads have revolutionized the advertising landscape, offering unparalleled opportunities for businesses to reach their target audiences with precision. Unlike traditional advertising, which often relies on broad demographic data and mass broadcasting, social media ads leverage the power of user data and platform algorithms to deliver personalized and highly relevant messages. This evolution has made advertising more efficient, measurable, and engaging.

The Advantages of Social Media Ads

One of the most significant advantages of social media advertising is its ability to target specific audiences with incredible accuracy. Platforms like Facebook, Instagram, X, LinkedIn, and TikTok provide advanced targeting options based on user demographics, interests, behaviors, and even past interactions with your brand. This granularity ensures that your ads reach the people most likely to be interested in your products or services, maximizing your return on investment.

Another key benefit is the ability to track and measure the performance of your ads in real time. Social media platforms offer robust analytics tools that provide insights into how your ads are performing, including metrics such as impressions, clicks, engagement, and conversions. This data allows you to adjust your campaigns on the fly, optimizing for better results and ensuring that your advertising budget is spent effectively.

Types of Social Media Ads

Social media platforms offer a variety of ad formats, each designed to achieve different objectives and engage users in unique ways. Understanding these formats can help you choose the best type of ad for your specific goals.

Image Ads: These are the simplest form of social media ads, featuring a single image and a short text description. They are effective for showcasing products, announcing promotions, or highlighting brand messages.

Video Ads: Videos can be more engaging than static images, allowing you to tell a story, demonstrate a product, or capture attention with motion and sound. Platforms like Facebook,

Instagram, and TikTok are particularly well-suited for video content.

Carousel Ads: These ads allow users to swipe through a series of images or videos within a single ad unit. Carousel ads are great for showcasing multiple products, detailing a step-by-step process, or telling a more comprehensive story.

Sponsored Posts: Also known as promoted posts, these are regular social media posts that you pay to reach a larger audience. Sponsored posts blend seamlessly into users' feeds, making them less intrusive and more likely to be engaged with.

Story Ads: These vertical ads appear in the stories section of platforms like Instagram, Facebook, and Snapchat. Story ads are immersive and can include interactive elements such as polls, swipe-up links, and augmented reality.

Messenger Ads: These ads appear within messaging apps like Facebook Messenger. They can initiate direct conversations with users, making them ideal for customer service, lead generation, and personalized marketing.

Crafting Effective Social Media Ads

Creating effective social media ads requires a blend of creativity, strategy, and data analysis. Start by clearly defining your campaign objectives. Are you looking to drive traffic to your website, generate leads, increase brand awareness, or boost sales? Your objective will shape your ad's content, format, and targeting strategy.

Next, focus on crafting compelling ad creatives. Your visuals should be eye-catching and aligned with your brand's aesthetic, while your copy should be concise, engaging, and include a clear call to action. A/B testing different versions of your ad can help you determine what resonates best with your audience.

Targeting is another crucial element. Utilize the advanced targeting options available on social media platforms to reach your ideal audience. This might include segmenting your audience by age, gender, location, interests, behaviors, or custom audiences based on your existing customer data.

Budgeting and Bidding Strategies

Effective budgeting and bidding strategies are essential for maximizing the impact of your social media ads. Start by setting a clear budget for your campaign, considering both your overall marketing budget and your specific goals for the campaign.

Most social media platforms use an auction system for ad placement, where advertisers bid for the opportunity to display their ads to the target audience. Decide on a bidding strategy that aligns with your objectives, whether it's cost-per-click (CPC), cost-per-impression (CPM), or cost-per-action (CPA).

Regularly monitor your ad spend and performance metrics. Adjust your bids and budget allocation based on the performance data to ensure you are getting the best possible return on your investment.

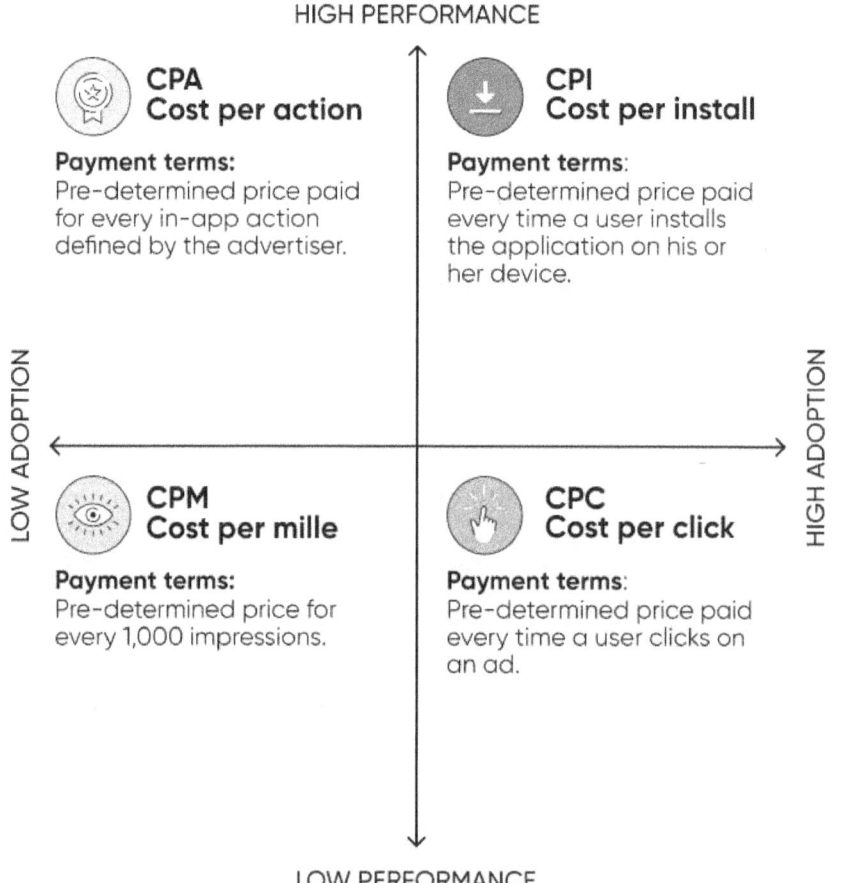

Comparing Advertising Models: CPC, CPM, CPI, and CPA. Source: appsflyer.com

The Future of Social Media Advertising

As social media continues to evolve, so too will the opportunities and challenges for advertisers. Emerging technologies like augmented reality (AR), virtual reality (VR), and artificial intelligence (AI) are poised to transform the way brands engage with consumers on social platforms. Staying ahead of these trends and continuously adapting your strategies will be key to maintaining a competitive edge.

In summary, social media ads offer a powerful and flexible tool for reaching your target audience, driving engagement, and achieving your business objectives. By understanding the different ad formats, crafting compelling creatives, leveraging precise targeting, and employing effective budgeting and bidding strategies, you can create impactful campaigns that deliver measurable results.

Creating Effective Ad Campaigns

Creating effective ad campaigns is essential for capturing your audience's attention and driving results. To achieve this, you need a combination of strategic planning, creative execution, and continuous optimization. Here's how to craft ad campaigns that stand out and deliver.

Understanding Your Audience

Before you start creating your ad campaign, it's crucial to understand who your target audience is. This involves analyzing demographics, interests, behaviors, and preferences. Knowing your audience allows you to tailor your message to their needs and desires, making your ads more relevant and compelling.

For example, if you are promoting a new line of eco-friendly products, understanding that your target audience values sustainability and environmentally friendly practices will help you craft a message that resonates with them. Use data from your social media insights, website analytics, and customer surveys to build a comprehensive profile of your ideal customer.

Setting Clear Objectives

Clear objectives guide your ad campaign and provide a way to measure its success. Whether your goal is to increase brand awareness, drive website traffic, generate leads, or boost sales, having a specific objective helps you design your campaign effectively.

For instance, if your goal is to drive website traffic, your ads should include compelling calls-to-action that encourage clicks, such as "Learn More" or "Shop Now." If you aim to increase brand awareness, focus on visually striking ads that highlight your brand's unique selling points.

Crafting Compelling Creative

The creative aspect of your ad campaign—images, videos, copy, and design—plays a pivotal role in capturing attention and conveying your message. Your creative should be visually appealing, consistent with your brand identity, and tailored to the platform you are using.

For example, Instagram ads often perform well with high-quality images or short videos, while LinkedIn ads might be more effective with professional, informative content. Ensure that your ad copy is clear, concise, and includes a strong call-to-action. Emotional appeals, humor, and storytelling can also enhance the impact of your ads.

Choosing the Right Platforms

Different social media platforms offer various ad formats and targeting options. Selecting the right platform for your campaign depends on where your audience spends their time and the nature of your product or service.

For instance, Facebook and Instagram are ideal for visually-driven consumer products, thanks to their rich media capabilities. LinkedIn is more suitable for B2B marketing, where professional content and networking are key. TikTok, with its short-form video content, is perfect for reaching younger audiences with creative, engaging ads.

Targeting Your Ads

Effective targeting ensures that your ads reach the right people. Use the targeting options provided by social media platforms to narrow down your audience based on demographics, interests, behaviors, and location.

For example, if you are advertising a new fitness app, you might target individuals interested in health and wellness, aged 18-35, living in urban areas. Advanced targeting options, like lookalike audiences, can help you reach new users who share characteristics with your existing customers, increasing the likelihood of conversion.

Budgeting and Bidding

Setting a budget and choosing a bidding strategy are critical components of your ad campaign. Your budget determines how much you are willing to spend, while your bidding strategy dictates how your budget is allocated to achieve your campaign goals.

For instance, you can set a daily or lifetime budget, and choose between cost-per-click (CPC), cost-per-impression (CPM), or cost-per-action (CPA) bidding strategies. Test different budget allocations and bidding strategies to find what works best for your campaign objectives. Monitor your spend regularly to ensure you are getting the best return on investment.

Monitoring and Optimization

Once your ad campaign is live, continuous monitoring and optimization are essential. Use the analytics tools provided by the social media platforms to track key metrics such as reach, engagement, click-through rates, and conversions.

For example, if you notice that certain ads are performing better than others, allocate more budget to those ads. A/B testing different versions of your ads—varying the images, headlines, and calls-to-action—can help identify the most effective elements. Regularly review your campaign performance and make data-driven adjustments to maximize results.

Leveraging Remarketing

Remarketing allows you to re-engage users who have previously interacted with your brand but haven't converted. By targeting these users with specific ads, you can remind them of your product or service and encourage them to take action.

For example, if a user visited your online store but didn't make a purchase, you can show them ads featuring the products they viewed, possibly with a special offer or discount. Remarketing helps you stay top-of-mind and can significantly increase conversion rates.

Creating effective ad campaigns involves understanding your audience, setting clear objectives, crafting compelling creative, choosing the right platforms, targeting your ads, budgeting wisely, and continuously monitoring and optimizing your efforts. By following these steps, you can design ad campaigns that capture attention, drive engagement, and achieve your marketing goals.

Budgeting and Bidding

Establishing a clear and realistic advertising budget is the first step toward a successful social media ad campaign. Start by defining your overall marketing budget and determining how much you can allocate to social media advertising. This allocation should be based on your business goals, the scale of your campaign, and the potential return on investment (ROI).

Consider the different stages of the customer journey and allocate your budget accordingly. For instance, you might spend more on awareness campaigns at the start and then shift to retargeting ads to convert engaged users. Balancing your budget across various stages ensures a comprehensive approach that nurtures leads through the entire sales funnel.

Understanding Bidding Strategies

Social media platforms use auction systems to determine which ads are shown to users. Advertisers bid for ad placements, and the highest bid doesn't always win. The platforms consider several factors, including the bid amount, ad quality, and relevance. Understanding different bidding strategies can help you maximize your ad performance while staying within budget.

Cost-Per-Click (CPC): CPC bidding charges you each time someone clicks on your ad. This strategy is ideal for driving traffic to your website or landing pages. It's particularly effective if you have compelling content that encourages clicks.

Cost-Per-Impression (CPM): CPM bidding charges you per thousand impressions. This approach is useful for increasing brand awareness and ensuring your ad is seen by a large audience. It's best when the goal is to boost visibility rather than direct engagement.

Cost-Per-Action (CPA): CPA bidding charges you when a user completes a specific action, such as making a purchase or filling out a form. This strategy is excellent for performance-driven campaigns where conversions are the primary goal. It ensures you're paying for actual results rather than just exposure.

Cost-Per-Engagement (CPE): CPE bidding focuses on actions such as likes, comments, shares, or other interactions with your ad. This method is effective for campaigns aiming to boost engagement and social proof.

Optimizing Your Bids

Optimizing your bids involves finding the right balance between competitiveness and cost-efficiency. Begin by setting a maximum bid that aligns with your budget and goals. Monitor your campaign performance closely, and be prepared to adjust your bids based on the results.

Analyze the cost and performance metrics regularly. If your ads are performing well and driving significant engagement or conversions, consider increasing your bid to enhance reach and results. Conversely, if your ads are underperforming, try lowering your bid or refining your targeting criteria to improve efficiency.

Utilizing Bid Caps and Automatic Bidding

Bid caps allow you to set a maximum bid amount for your campaigns, ensuring you don't overspend on individual clicks or impressions. This approach gives you greater control over your budget and prevents unexpected costs.

Automatic bidding is another option, where the social media platform adjusts your bids in real-time to achieve the best possible results within your budget. This method can be particularly useful for advertisers who are new to social media advertising or those who prefer a hands-off approach. Automatic bidding leverages the platform's algorithms to optimize bids based on performance data, saving you time and effort.

Budget Allocation Strategies

Effective budget allocation is crucial for maximizing your ad spend. Consider testing various allocation strategies to determine what works best for your business. One approach is to start with a small budget and gradually increase it as you gather data and see positive results. This method minimizes risk and allows you to optimize your campaigns based on real-world performance.

Another strategy is to allocate a portion of your budget to experimentation. Testing different ad formats, creatives, and targeting options can reveal valuable insights and opportunities for improvement. Allocate a fixed percentage of your budget to A/B testing to continually refine your campaigns.

Monitoring and Adjusting Your Budget

Continuous monitoring and adjustment of your budget and bids are essential for maintaining an effective social media ad campaign. Use analytics tools to track key performance indicators such as cost per click, conversion rate, and return on ad spend. Regularly review this data to identify trends and make informed decisions about budget adjustments.

If a particular ad set or campaign is underperforming, reallocate the budget to higher-performing initiatives. Conversely, if you identify a campaign that is driving exceptional results, consider increasing its budget to maximize impact.

Budgeting and bidding are dynamic processes that require careful planning, ongoing monitoring, and strategic adjustments. By understanding your options and continuously optimizing your approach, you can ensure your social media ad campaigns deliver the best possible results while staying within budget.

Measuring Ad Performance

Effective ad campaigns rely on continuous assessment to ensure they are meeting their goals and delivering value. Measuring ad performance is essential for understanding the impact of your efforts and making data-driven decisions to optimize future campaigns. Here's how to evaluate the success of your ads and refine your strategies for better results.

Defining Key Metrics

To measure ad performance, start by defining the key metrics that align with your campaign objectives. These metrics will vary depending on your goals, such as increasing brand awareness, driving traffic, generating leads, or boosting sales.

For instance, if your objective is to drive website traffic, key metrics might include click-through rates (CTR), the number of clicks, and landing page views. If your goal is to increase sales, you should focus on conversion rates, cost per acquisition (CPA), and return on ad spend (ROAS). Clearly identifying these metrics provides a benchmark for evaluating your campaign's success.

Tracking Engagement

Engagement metrics are crucial for understanding how your audience interacts with your ads. These metrics include likes, comments, shares, and overall engagement rates. High engagement indicates that your content resonates with your audience, fostering a connection that can lead to higher conversion rates.

For example, if a Facebook ad receives a significant number of shares and comments, it suggests that the content is engaging and relevant. Monitoring these interactions helps you identify which aspects of your ads are effective and which may need adjustment.

Analyzing Click-Through Rates

Click-through rate (CTR) is a fundamental metric that measures the percentage of people who click on your ad after seeing it. A high CTR indicates that your ad is compelling and effectively driving traffic to your website or landing page. Conversely, a low CTR may suggest that your ad copy, visuals, or targeting need improvement.

Regularly analyze your CTR to gauge the effectiveness of your ads. For instance, if an Instagram ad with a stunning image and a clear call-to-action has a high CTR, it indicates that these elements are working well. Use these insights to refine your future ads for better performance.

Evaluating Conversion Rates

Conversion rate is one of the most critical metrics, particularly for campaigns aimed at driving specific actions such as purchases, sign-ups, or downloads. It measures the percentage of users who take the desired action after clicking on your ad.

To improve your conversion rate, analyze the entire customer journey from the ad click to the final conversion. If a significant drop-off occurs at any stage, identify potential barriers such as a confusing landing page or a lengthy checkout process.

Optimizing these elements can significantly boost your conversion rates.

Monitoring Return on Ad Spend

Return on ad spend (ROAS) measures the revenue generated for every dollar spent on advertising. It provides a clear picture of the financial effectiveness of your ad campaigns. A high ROAS indicates that your ads are generating substantial revenue relative to their cost, while a low ROAS suggests the need for strategic adjustments.

For example, if you spend $1,000 on a Facebook ad campaign and generate $5,000 in sales, your ROAS is 5:1. Monitoring this metric helps you allocate your budget more effectively, investing more in high-performing campaigns and adjusting or discontinuing those that underperform.

Using Analytics Tools

Various analytics tools can help you track and measure your ad performance. Platforms like Google Analytics, Facebook Insights, and Instagram Analytics provide detailed reports on key metrics, helping you understand your ad's impact and audience behavior.

For instance, Google Analytics can show you how users from different ad campaigns interact with your website, revealing valuable insights into user behavior and conversion paths. Utilizing these tools allows you to make informed decisions based on real-time data.

Conducting A/B Testing

A/B testing, or split testing, involves running two variations of an ad to determine which performs better. This method is invaluable for optimizing ad elements such as headlines, images, calls-to-action, and targeting options.

For example, you might create two versions of a LinkedIn ad with different headlines. By comparing their performance, you can identify which headline resonates more with your audience and apply this insight to future campaigns. Regular A/B testing helps you continually refine your ads for maximum effectiveness.

Adjusting Based on Insights

Effective ad measurement isn't just about gathering data; it's about using that data to make strategic adjustments. Regularly review your metrics to identify trends and areas for improvement. If certain ads are underperforming, analyze the data to understand why and adjust your strategy accordingly.

For instance, if your engagement rates are high but conversions are low, you may need to refine your landing page or offer. Conversely, if your ads are generating clicks but low engagement, reconsider your targeting or ad creative. Continuous optimization based on insights ensures that your campaigns remain dynamic and effective.

Measuring ad performance involves defining key metrics, tracking engagement, analyzing click-through and conversion rates, monitoring return on ad spend, using analytics tools, conducting A/B testing, and making data-driven adjustments. This comprehensive approach allows you to assess your campaigns accurately and optimize them for better results, ensuring your marketing efforts are both efficient and impactful.

Chapter 8: Automation and Efficiency

Social Media Management Tools

Managing social media effectively can be a daunting task, especially as your presence and engagement grow. Social media management tools are designed to streamline the process, making it easier to create, schedule, and analyze your content. These tools help you maintain a consistent posting schedule, engage with your audience efficiently, and gain valuable insights into your performance.

Popular Social Media Management Tools

Several social media management tools stand out for their features, ease of use, and ability to handle various aspects of social media marketing. Here, we explore some of the most popular ones and how they can benefit your strategy.

Hootsuite: One of the earliest and most comprehensive social media management platforms, Hootsuite supports scheduling and posting across multiple social networks from one dashboard. It also offers powerful analytics to track your performance and measure the effectiveness of your campaigns. Hootsuite's team collaboration features make it ideal for larger organizations managing multiple accounts.

Buffer: Known for its simplicity and user-friendly interface, Buffer allows you to schedule posts, track engagement, and analyze performance across various social media platforms. Buffer's focus on simplicity makes it a great choice for small businesses and individual marketers looking for an easy way to manage their social media presence.

Sprout Social: This tool combines social media management with customer relationship management (CRM) capabilities. Sprout Social offers robust analytics, scheduling, and engagement tools, as well as advanced features like social listening and customer care. Its CRM features help you understand your audience better and build stronger relationships.

Later: Specializing in visual content, Later is an excellent tool for managing Instagram, Pinterest, Facebook, and X. It offers drag-and-drop scheduling, a visual content calendar, and analytics tailored to visual platforms. Later's focus on visual scheduling makes it particularly useful for brands that rely heavily on images and videos.

Canva: While primarily a design tool, Canva's social media integration allows you to create stunning graphics and schedule them directly to your social media platforms. Canva is perfect for marketers who need a quick and easy way to produce high-quality visual content without professional design skills.

Features to Look For

When choosing a social media management tool, consider the features that will best support your strategy and workflow. Here are some key features to look for:

Scheduling and Publishing: The ability to schedule posts in advance ensures you maintain a consistent posting schedule without having to manually post content in real-time. Look for tools that support multiple social media platforms and offer a visual content calendar.

Analytics and Reporting: Comprehensive analytics help you track performance, measure engagement, and understand your audience's behavior. Detailed reports can provide insights into what's working and what needs improvement, allowing you to refine your strategy.

Engagement Tools: Effective social media management includes monitoring and responding to comments, messages, and mentions. Tools with robust engagement features help you stay on top of interactions and foster stronger relationships with your audience.

Content Creation: Integrated content creation tools, like those offered by Canva, can streamline the process of producing engaging visuals. Look for features that allow you to design, edit, and publish content from within the platform.

Team Collaboration: If you're working with a team, collaboration features are essential. Tools that allow multiple users, task assignments, and approval workflows can improve efficiency and ensure consistency in your social media efforts.

Social Listening: Understanding what people are saying about your brand, competitors, and industry is crucial. Social listening tools monitor mentions and keywords across social media, providing valuable insights and opportunities to engage with your audience.

Maximizing the Benefits of Management Tools

To get the most out of your social media management tools, integrate them fully into your workflow. Regularly review the analytics to understand trends and adjust your strategy accordingly. Use the scheduling features to plan your content ahead of time, ensuring a steady flow of posts without the stress of last-minute planning.

Engage actively with your audience by leveraging the engagement tools provided. Respond to comments and messages promptly, and participate in conversations to build a stronger community around your brand. Utilize the social listening features to stay informed about industry trends and customer sentiments, allowing you to react quickly and appropriately.

Social media management tools are invaluable for streamlining your processes, improving efficiency, and gaining deeper insights into your performance. By selecting the right tools and fully integrating them into your strategy, you can enhance your social media marketing efforts and achieve your business goals more effectively.

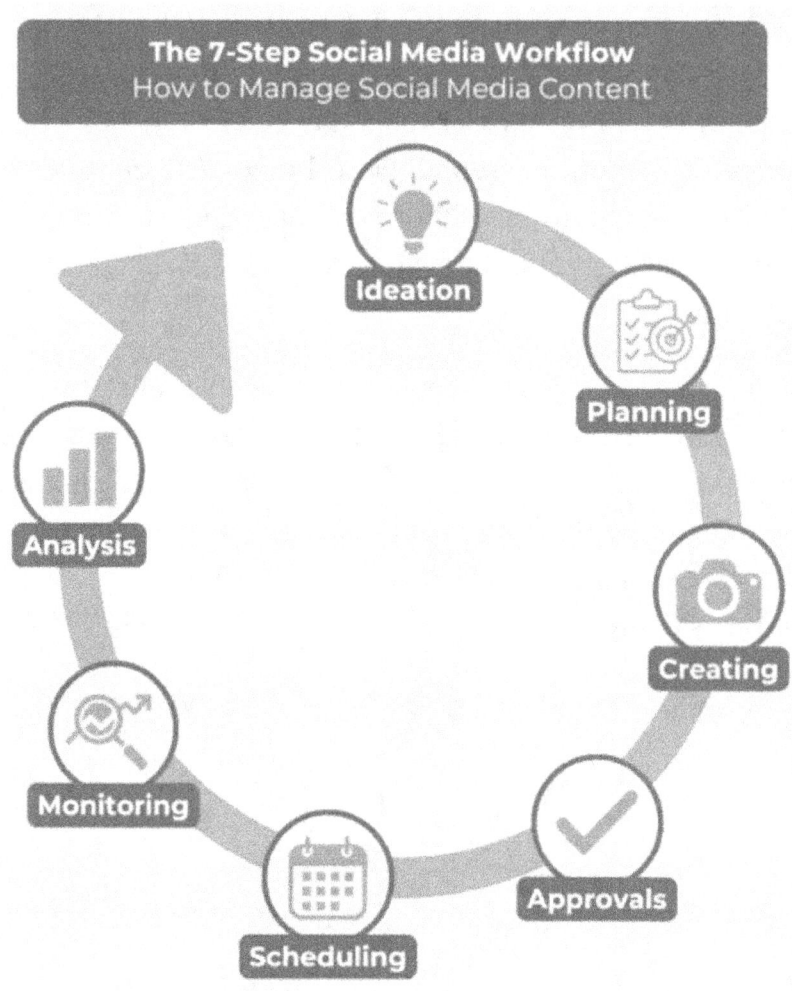

The 7-Step Social Media Workflow for Content Management.
Source: loomly.com

Creating an Automated Workflow

In the fast-paced world of social media marketing, efficiency is key. Creating an automated workflow can save time, reduce errors, and ensure consistency across your campaigns. Automation allows you to focus on strategy and creativity, while routine tasks are handled seamlessly. Here's how to develop an effective automated workflow for your social media marketing efforts.

Identifying Tasks for Automation

The first step in creating an automated workflow is identifying which tasks can be automated. These typically include repetitive and time-consuming activities such as content scheduling, social media posting, and data collection.

For instance, scheduling posts in advance can be automated using tools like Hootsuite or Buffer. These platforms allow you to plan and queue your content, ensuring that posts are published at optimal times without manual intervention. This consistency helps maintain your brand presence and engagement levels.

Choosing the Right Tools

Selecting the right automation tools is crucial for building an effective workflow. There are numerous tools available, each with unique features designed to streamline different aspects of social media management.

For example, tools like Sprout Social and Later can automate post scheduling and provide analytics to track performance. Zapier can connect various apps and automate complex workflows by triggering actions across different platforms. Choosing tools that integrate well with your existing systems and meet your specific needs is essential.

Setting Up Content Calendars

A content calendar is a vital component of an automated workflow. It helps you organize and plan your posts in advance, ensuring a steady stream of content that aligns with your marketing strategy.

Use your chosen automation tool to create a calendar where you can schedule posts weeks or even months ahead. This approach not only saves time but also allows you to visualize your content distribution, ensuring a balanced mix of promotions, engagement posts, and informative content.

Automating Engagement

Engagement is a critical aspect of social media marketing, and while it should not be fully automated, certain elements can be streamlined. Tools like Chatfuel for Facebook Messenger or ManyChat can automate initial customer interactions, providing instant responses to common inquiries.

For example, a chatbot can greet visitors, answer frequently asked questions, or direct users to specific resources, ensuring that your audience receives timely responses even when your team is offline. This initial engagement can be followed up by personal interactions to maintain a human touch.

Monitoring and Analytics

Automation tools can also help you keep track of your social media performance by gathering and analyzing data. Tools like Google Analytics, Sprinklr, and Socialbakers can automatically collect metrics and generate reports, providing insights into your campaigns' effectiveness.

Set up these tools to monitor key performance indicators (KPIs) such as engagement rates, click-through rates, and conversions. Regularly reviewing these automated reports can help you identify trends and make data-driven decisions to optimize your strategy.

Streamlining Approval Processes

In larger teams, content approval processes can be a bottleneck. Automating these workflows can ensure a smoother and faster process. Tools like Trello or Asana can automate task assignments and approval requests, notifying team members when their input or approval is needed.

For instance, you can set up a workflow where a social media post draft is automatically sent to a manager for review. Once approved, the post is then scheduled for publishing. This reduces delays and keeps your content pipeline moving efficiently.

Implementing Automated Alerts

Automated alerts can help you stay on top of important activities without constantly monitoring your social media channels. Tools like Mention or Brand24 can send notifications when your brand is mentioned, allowing you to respond promptly to customer feedback or emerging trends.

Set up alerts for specific keywords, hashtags, or mentions related to your brand. This proactive approach enables you to engage with your audience in real time, address issues quickly, and capitalize on opportunities as they arise.

Continuous Improvement

Automation is not a set-and-forget solution. Regularly review and refine your automated workflows to ensure they are functioning optimally and meeting your goals. Gather feedback from your team and monitor the performance of your automated processes to identify areas for improvement.

For instance, if you notice that certain automated responses are not resonating with your audience, adjust the messaging to be more effective. Continuously updating and optimizing your workflows ensures that your automation efforts remain aligned with your evolving business objectives.

Creating an automated workflow involves identifying tasks for automation, choosing the right tools, setting up content calendars, automating engagement, monitoring performance, streamlining approval processes, implementing alerts, and continuously refining your processes. By effectively automating routine tasks, you can focus on strategic initiatives, enhance efficiency, and ensure a consistent and engaging social media presence.

Maintaining Human Touch

In an era dominated by automation and algorithms, maintaining a human touch in your social media interactions is crucial. Authenticity builds trust and fosters deeper connections with your audience. People want to engage with brands that feel personal and genuine, not robotic and detached. Ensuring that your brand's voice remains warm and relatable can significantly enhance your social media presence.

Personalizing Interactions

Personalization is key to maintaining a human touch. Addressing your audience by their names, referencing past interactions, and tailoring responses to their specific questions or comments shows that you see them as individuals, not just numbers. This approach can be particularly effective in customer service interactions, where a personalized touch can turn a neutral or negative experience into a positive one.

For instance, instead of a generic response like "Thank you for your comment," try "Thank you, Sarah, for your thoughtful feedback on our new product. We're glad you enjoyed it!" This small effort in personalizing responses can make a big difference in how your audience perceives your brand.

Showing Empathy and Understanding

Empathy is another critical component of maintaining a human touch. Show that you understand and care about your audience's needs, concerns, and experiences. When responding to customer complaints or issues, acknowledge their feelings and provide solutions that demonstrate your commitment to their satisfaction.

For example, if a customer expresses frustration about a delayed shipment, an empathetic response might be, "We understand how frustrating it can be to wait for your order, and we apologize for the delay. We're working hard to resolve this issue and will keep you updated on your order's status." Such responses show that you value your customers' feelings and are dedicated to addressing their concerns.

Sharing Behind-the-Scenes Content

Giving your audience a glimpse behind the scenes of your business can humanize your brand and make it more relatable. Share stories about your team, your work environment, and the processes behind your products or services. This transparency helps build trust and shows the human side of your brand.

For example, you might post a video tour of your office, introduce team members in social media posts, or share stories about how your products are made. These behind-the-scenes looks can foster a sense of connection and loyalty among your audience.

Engaging in Real Conversations

Engagement is not just about responding to comments and messages; it's about having real conversations with your audience. Ask open-ended questions, encourage discussions, and participate actively in those conversations. Show that you are genuinely interested in what your audience has to say.

When someone comments on your post, take the opportunity to engage in a meaningful dialogue. If a customer shares a positive experience with your product, thank them and ask for more details about their experience. If someone has a question, provide a thoughtful and detailed answer. These interactions can help build a vibrant and engaged community around your brand.

Balancing Automation with Personal Touch

While automation can streamline many aspects of social media management, it's essential to balance it with personal interactions. Use automated tools for routine tasks like scheduling posts and gathering analytics, but ensure that your direct engagements with your audience are personal and genuine.

Automated responses can sometimes come across as cold and impersonal. Whenever possible, prioritize human responses, especially for customer service issues or more complex inquiries. If you use chatbots or automated messages, make sure they are well-designed to provide value and lead seamlessly to human interaction when needed.

Highlighting User-Generated Content

Featuring user-generated content is a powerful way to show appreciation for your audience and highlight the human aspect of your brand. Share posts, photos, and stories from your customers, and give them credit for their contributions. This not only makes your content more relatable but also encourages others to engage with your brand.

For instance, if a customer shares a photo of themselves using your product, repost it with a thank you message and a tag to their profile. This kind of recognition makes your customers feel valued and promotes a sense of community.

Maintaining a human touch in your social media interactions is about being authentic, empathetic, and genuinely engaged with your audience. By personalizing interactions, showing empathy, sharing behind-the-scenes content, engaging in real conversations, balancing automation, and highlighting user-generated content, you can create a more relatable and trustworthy brand presence that resonates deeply with your audience.

Review and Optimization

Reviewing and optimizing your social media strategy is crucial for achieving continuous improvement and sustained success. Regular evaluation allows you to understand what's working, identify areas for improvement, and adjust your tactics to better align with your goals. Here's how to effectively review and optimize your social media efforts.

Analyzing Performance Metrics

The first step in the review process is to analyze performance metrics. These metrics provide a clear picture of how well your social media campaigns are performing. Key metrics include engagement rates, click-through rates (CTR), conversion rates, and overall reach.

For instance, if a particular post received high engagement but low click-through rates, it suggests that while the content was interesting, the call-to-action may need improvement. Analyzing such metrics helps pinpoint specific elements that require adjustment.

Gathering Insights from Analytics Tools

Using analytics tools can significantly enhance your review process. Tools like Google Analytics, Hootsuite, and Sprout Social offer detailed insights into your social media performance. These platforms provide data on user behavior, engagement patterns, and content effectiveness.

For example, Google Analytics can show how social media traffic behaves on your website, including bounce rates and conversion paths. Understanding these patterns helps you identify which types of content drive the most valuable traffic and conversions.

Evaluating Content Performance

Assessing the performance of your content is essential for optimization. Identify which types of posts resonate most with your audience. Look at factors such as content format (videos, images, text), topics, and posting times.

For instance, if video content consistently outperforms other formats, consider increasing your focus on video production. Additionally, analyzing which topics generate the most engagement can help you tailor your content strategy to meet your audience's interests.

A/B Testing for Improvement

A/B testing is a powerful technique for optimization. By comparing two versions of an ad or post, you can determine which one performs better and why. Test different headlines, images, calls-to-action, and posting times to see what drives the best results.

For example, you might test two different headlines for the same blog post to see which one attracts more clicks. The insights gained from A/B testing can inform future content creation and campaign strategies.

Adjusting Based on Feedback

Customer feedback is invaluable for optimization. Monitor comments, messages, and reviews to understand your audience's perceptions and experiences. This feedback provides direct insights into what your audience likes or dislikes about your content and brand.

For instance, if customers frequently mention slow response times, you might need to improve your social media engagement strategy. Responding to feedback not only enhances customer satisfaction but also helps refine your overall approach.

Refining Targeting Strategies

Effective targeting is crucial for reaching the right audience. Regularly review and adjust your targeting strategies based on performance data. Identify which demographics, interests, and behaviors yield the best results and refine your targeting criteria accordingly.

For example, if you notice that a specific age group engages more with your content, tailor your ads to appeal more directly to that demographic. Continuous refinement of your targeting strategies ensures your content reaches the most relevant audience.

Monitoring Competitor Activity

Keeping an eye on your competitors can provide valuable insights. Analyze their social media strategies, content performance, and audience engagement. Understanding what works well for your competitors can help you identify opportunities and gaps in your own strategy.

For instance, if a competitor's campaign on sustainability gains significant traction, consider how you might incorporate similar themes that align with your brand values. Competitive analysis helps you stay ahead and innovate based on industry trends.

Implementing Continuous Improvement

Optimization is an ongoing process. Regularly review your social media performance, gather insights, and make necessary adjustments. Set aside time each month or quarter to assess your strategy and implement changes.

For example, schedule monthly reviews to analyze recent campaign data, test new ideas, and adjust your content calendar. Continuous improvement ensures that your social media efforts remain effective and aligned with your evolving business goals.

Reviewing and optimizing your social media strategy involves analyzing performance metrics, gathering insights from analytics tools, evaluating content performance, conducting

A/B tests, adjusting based on feedback, refining targeting strategies, monitoring competitor activity, and committing to continuous improvement. By following these steps, you can enhance your social media presence and achieve greater success in your marketing efforts.

Chapter 9: Adapting to Platform Changes

Keeping Up with Algorithm Updates

Social media platforms frequently update their algorithms to improve user experience and engagement. These changes can significantly impact how your content is distributed and seen by your audience. Staying informed about these updates is crucial for maintaining an effective social media strategy and ensuring that your content continues to reach its intended audience.

Understanding Algorithm Basics

Algorithms determine what content users see in their feeds based on various factors such as relevance, engagement, and user behavior. Each platform has its own set of rules and priorities, which can change regularly. For example, Facebook's algorithm prioritizes content from friends and family, while Instagram's focuses on user engagement and interests. Understanding these foundational principles helps you adapt your content strategy accordingly.

Staying Informed

Keeping up with algorithm updates requires a proactive approach. Follow official announcements from social media platforms, subscribe to industry blogs, and join relevant online communities. Websites like Social Media Examiner, TechCrunch, and the official blogs of Facebook, X, and LinkedIn often provide timely updates and insights.

Additionally, attending webinars, conferences, and workshops can offer valuable information and expert opinions on the latest algorithm changes. Networking with other social media professionals can also provide practical tips and strategies for adapting to these changes.

Adapting Your Content Strategy

Algorithm updates often require adjustments to your content strategy. Analyze how changes affect your content's performance by closely monitoring key metrics such as reach, engagement, and impressions. If you notice a decline in performance, experiment with different types of content, posting times, and engagement techniques to see what resonates best with the updated algorithm.

For instance, if a platform begins prioritizing video content, consider increasing your production of high-quality videos. If engagement becomes a more critical factor, focus on creating interactive content that encourages likes, comments, and shares.

Leveraging Platform-Specific Features

Social media platforms frequently introduce new features that align with their latest algorithm updates. Embracing these features can enhance your visibility and engagement. For example, Instagram's algorithm favors accounts that use its various features like Stories, IGTV, and Reels. Similarly, LinkedIn's algorithm boosts content that includes native videos and documents.

Staying ahead of these features not only helps you comply with the algorithm but also shows your audience that you are active and innovative. Experiment with new formats and track their performance to refine your approach.

Engaging Authentically

Despite algorithm changes, authentic engagement remains a constant priority across all platforms. Algorithms favor content that generates meaningful interactions, such as comments, shares, and extended viewing times. Building genuine relationships with your audience by responding to comments, asking questions, and fostering community discussions can help your content perform better.

Avoid shortcuts like engagement pods or buying likes and followers, as these can lead to penalties and reduce your content's reach. Focus on organic growth through valuable content and sincere interactions.

Utilizing Analytics and Insights

Regularly reviewing your analytics and insights helps you understand the impact of algorithm updates on your content. Use tools provided by social media platforms, such as Facebook Insights, X Analytics, and Instagram Insights, to gather data on your performance. Analyze this data to identify trends, strengths, and areas for improvement.

For example, if your reach decreases after an algorithm update, look at the types of content that still perform well and try to replicate those successes. Use A/B testing to experiment with different content strategies and find what works best under the new algorithm rules.

Continuous Learning and Adaptation

The world of social media is ever-evolving, and staying relevant requires continuous learning and adaptation. Set aside time regularly to educate yourself about the latest trends, tools, and best practices in social media marketing. Join professional groups, follow industry leaders, and participate in discussions to keep your knowledge up to date.

Be prepared to pivot your strategy as needed. Flexibility and responsiveness are key to thriving in an environment where algorithms can change overnight. By remaining informed and adaptable, you can navigate algorithm updates effectively and maintain a strong presence on social media.

Keeping up with algorithm updates is an ongoing process that demands vigilance, adaptability, and a commitment to continuous improvement. By understanding the basics, staying informed, adapting your strategy, leveraging new features, engaging authentically, utilizing analytics, and continuously learning, you can ensure that your social media efforts remain effective and impactful.

Adapting Content Strategy

A dynamic content strategy is essential in the ever-changing landscape of social media marketing. Adapting your strategy to align with evolving trends, audience preferences, and platform algorithms ensures that your content remains relevant and engaging. Here's how to effectively adapt your content strategy for sustained success.

Staying Current with Trends

Keeping up with trends is crucial for maintaining a vibrant and engaging content strategy. Social media trends can change rapidly, influenced by cultural events, technological advancements, and shifts in user behavior. Regularly monitoring these trends helps you stay ahead and incorporate relevant themes into your content.

For example, the rise of short-form video content on platforms like TikTok and Instagram Reels has prompted many brands to adjust their strategies. By creating short, engaging videos that align with these trends, you can capture the attention of a broader audience and increase your reach.

Understanding Audience Preferences

Your audience's preferences are constantly evolving, and understanding these changes is key to maintaining engagement. Regularly analyze data from your social media platforms to identify what types of content resonate most with your followers.

For instance, if you notice that your audience engages more with behind-the-scenes content or user-generated posts, consider incorporating more of these into your strategy. Tailoring your content to meet your audience's preferences ensures that you provide value and maintain their interest.

Experimenting with Content Formats

Diversifying your content formats keeps your strategy fresh and engaging. Experiment with different types of content, such as videos, infographics, podcasts, and interactive posts, to see what works best for your audience.

For example, if you typically post static images, try adding more video content to your mix. Videos can offer a more dynamic and immersive experience, potentially increasing engagement and shares. Regular experimentation allows you to discover new ways to connect with your audience and keep your content strategy innovative.

Analyzing Platform Algorithms

Social media platforms frequently update their algorithms, which can impact the visibility of your content. Staying informed about these changes and adjusting your strategy accordingly is crucial for maintaining reach and engagement.

For instance, if Instagram updates its algorithm to favor Reels, incorporating more Reels into your content plan can help boost your visibility. Understanding how each platform's algorithm prioritizes content enables you to optimize your posts for maximum exposure.

Leveraging Data Insights

Data-driven insights are invaluable for adapting your content strategy. Use analytics tools to track the performance of your posts and campaigns, identifying what works and what doesn't. This data helps you make informed decisions and refine your approach.

For example, if your analytics show that posts with questions receive higher engagement, you might incorporate more interactive content that encourages audience participation. Continuously leveraging data insights ensures that your content strategy is based on real performance rather than assumptions.

Responding to Feedback

Audience feedback is a direct indicator of how well your content is received. Pay attention to comments, messages, and reviews to understand what your audience enjoys and what they'd like to see more of. Incorporating this feedback into your strategy can improve your content's relevance and appeal.

For instance, if followers frequently request tutorials or how-to guides, consider adding this type of content to your lineup. Responding to feedback not only enhances your content but also shows your audience that you value their input.

Adapting to Seasonal and Event-Based Changes

Seasonal trends and major events offer opportunities to adapt your content strategy and stay relevant. Tailoring your content to align with holidays, industry events, or cultural moments can increase engagement and resonance.

For example, during the holiday season, you might create festive content that ties into the celebratory mood, such as holiday gift guides or special promotions. Adapting your strategy to these cyclical changes helps keep your content timely and engaging.

Streamlining Content Creation Processes

Efficiency in content creation is essential for maintaining a consistent output. Streamlining your processes through planning and automation can free up time for strategic adjustments and creative experimentation.

For example, using a content calendar to plan your posts in advance ensures a steady flow of content while allowing flexibility to incorporate new ideas. Automation tools can handle repetitive tasks, such as scheduling posts, giving you more time to focus on optimizing your strategy.

Adapting your content strategy involves staying current with trends, understanding audience preferences, experimenting with formats, analyzing platform algorithms, leveraging data insights, responding to feedback, adapting to seasonal changes, and streamlining content creation processes. By continually refining your approach, you can ensure that your content remains relevant, engaging, and effective in achieving your marketing goals.

Testing and Experimentation

Testing and experimentation are essential for discovering what resonates with your audience and optimizing your strategies for better performance. By systematically experimenting with different elements of your campaigns, you can uncover valuable insights and continuously improve your results.

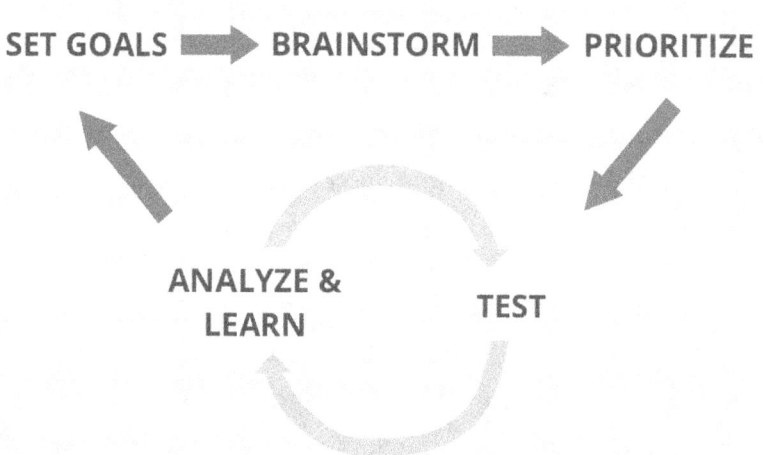

How to Run Effective Social Media Experiments. Source: buffer.com

Designing Effective Experiments

Effective experimentation begins with a clear hypothesis. Identify a specific aspect of your social media strategy that you want to test. This could be the type of content, posting times, headlines, images, or calls to action. Define what you hope to learn from the experiment and what metrics you will use to measure success.

For example, you might hypothesize that videos will generate higher engagement than static images. To test this, you could create similar content in both formats and compare the performance metrics, such as likes, shares, comments, and view duration.

A/B Testing

A/B testing, also known as split testing, is a common method for experimenting with different variables. In an A/B test, you create two versions of a single element and show them to different segments of your audience to see which performs better. This approach allows you to isolate the impact of one variable at a time, making it easier to determine what works best.

For instance, if you want to test the effectiveness of two different headlines, you would create two identical posts with only the headlines changed. By comparing the engagement rates of each post, you can identify which headline is more compelling to your audience.

Iterative Testing

Testing should be an ongoing process, not a one-time event. Iterative testing involves making small, incremental changes to your strategy based on the results of previous experiments. This continuous improvement approach helps you refine your tactics over time and adapt to changing audience preferences.

After conducting an initial A/B test, use the winning variant as your new baseline. Then, introduce another variable to test against this baseline. This iterative process allows you to build on your successes and progressively optimize your social media strategy.

Leveraging Analytics for Insights

Analytics play a crucial role in testing and experimentation. Use the analytics tools provided by social media platforms to track the performance of your experiments. Pay attention to key metrics such as engagement rates, click-through rates, conversion rates, and overall reach.

By analyzing this data, you can identify patterns and trends that inform your future experiments. For example, if your data shows that posts with questions generate more comments, you might decide to incorporate more question-based content into your strategy.

Testing Different Content Formats

Content format is a critical variable in social media marketing. Experimenting with different formats—such as videos, images, carousels, stories, and live streams—can reveal which types resonate most with your audience.

Create content in various formats and monitor their performance. For instance, you might find that short videos on Instagram Reels attract more views and engagement compared to traditional photo posts. Use these insights to tailor your content strategy to better align with your audience's preferences.

Timing and Frequency

The timing and frequency of your posts can significantly impact their performance. Experiment with posting at different times of the day and on different days of the week to see when your audience is most active and engaged.

Similarly, test different posting frequencies to find the optimal balance between staying top-of-mind and overwhelming your audience. Analyzing the performance of posts published at various intervals can help you identify the best schedule for maximizing reach and engagement.

Experimenting with Ad Campaigns

Paid social media advertising offers another avenue for experimentation. Test different ad creatives, targeting options, and bidding strategies to determine what drives the best results. Use A/B testing to compare the effectiveness of various ad elements, such as images, headlines, and calls to action.

Adjust your ad campaigns based on the insights gained from these experiments. For example, if an ad targeting a specific demographic outperforms others, you might allocate more of your budget to similar audiences.

Documenting and Sharing Findings

Keep detailed records of your experiments, including the hypotheses, variables tested, results, and insights gained. This documentation not only helps you track your progress but also allows you to share valuable learnings with your team.

Regularly review and discuss your findings to ensure that everyone is aligned and can contribute to refining your strategy.

Collaborative analysis can lead to new ideas and more effective approaches to social media marketing.

Testing and experimentation are essential for staying agile and responsive in the ever-evolving landscape of social media. By designing effective experiments, leveraging analytics, and continuously refining your strategy, you can uncover powerful insights and drive better results for your brand.

Learning from Success and Failure

In the dynamic field of social media marketing, both success and failure provide invaluable lessons. Each campaign, whether it hits the mark or falls short, offers insights that can shape future strategies. Embracing both triumphs and setbacks as learning opportunities is essential for growth and continuous improvement. Here's how to effectively learn from your successes and failures.

Analyzing Successful Campaigns

When a campaign performs exceptionally well, it's crucial to understand the elements that contributed to its success. Start by identifying the key metrics that indicate success, such as high engagement rates, increased followers, or significant conversions.

For example, if a particular Instagram campaign results in a substantial increase in followers and engagement, analyze the content, timing, and format used. Was it a series of compelling stories, high-quality images, or interactive posts? Understanding these factors helps replicate success in future campaigns.

Additionally, consider the context of the campaign. Was there a specific event, trend, or holiday that boosted its performance? Identifying these external factors can help you time future campaigns more effectively.

Understanding Failures

Failures can be disheartening, but they are equally important in refining your strategy. When a campaign doesn't meet expectations, delve into the data to understand why. Look at metrics such as low engagement, high bounce rates, or poor conversion rates.

For instance, if a Facebook ad campaign fails to generate clicks, examine the ad's creative elements, target audience, and placement. Was the messaging clear and compelling? Did it reach the right audience? Were there technical issues that might have hindered performance? By identifying these issues, you can avoid similar pitfalls in the future.

Gathering Feedback

Direct feedback from your audience provides valuable insights into what worked and what didn't. Monitor comments, messages, and reviews to gather this information. Positive feedback can highlight strengths to build on, while negative feedback can pinpoint areas for improvement.

For example, if users praise the visual aesthetics of your posts but criticize the lack of useful information, you might focus on incorporating more informative content without compromising on visual appeal. Listening to your audience ensures that your strategy remains aligned with their preferences and expectations.

Conducting Post-Mortem Analysis

After completing a campaign, conducting a thorough post-mortem analysis helps consolidate learnings. Gather your team to review the campaign's performance, discussing what went well and what didn't. This collaborative approach can uncover insights that might not be apparent from data alone.

For instance, team members might provide perspectives on internal processes that impacted the campaign, such as communication gaps or resource constraints. Addressing these internal factors can improve efficiency and effectiveness in future campaigns.

Implementing Changes

The ultimate goal of learning from success and failure is to implement changes that enhance future performance. Use the insights gained from your analysis to refine your strategies, processes, and content.

For example, if you learn that your audience responds well to video content, allocate more resources to video production. If targeting issues are identified, adjust your audience segmentation to ensure your ads reach the right people. Continually iterating based on these learnings fosters a culture of improvement.

Documenting Lessons Learned

Maintaining a record of lessons learned from each campaign helps institutionalize knowledge within your team. Create a document or database where you record key takeaways, successful tactics, and common pitfalls. This resource can serve as a reference for planning future campaigns, ensuring that past insights are readily accessible.

For instance, a documented lesson might include the finding that posts with user-generated content receive higher engagement. Future campaigns can then prioritize incorporating user-generated content to replicate this success.

Staying Adaptable

The landscape of social media is constantly evolving, and what works today might not work tomorrow. Staying adaptable and open to change is crucial. Regularly revisit and update your strategies based on new learnings and emerging trends.

For example, if a new social media platform gains popularity among your target audience, be prepared to explore and adapt your strategy to include that platform. Flexibility ensures that your marketing efforts remain relevant and effective in a shifting environment.

Learning from success and failure involves analyzing performance, understanding context, gathering feedback, conducting post-mortem analyses, implementing changes, documenting lessons, and staying adaptable. By embracing these practices, you can continuously refine your social media strategy, turning both triumphs and setbacks into stepping stones for ongoing improvement and success.

Chapter 10: Future Trends in Social Media Marketing

The Role of AI and Machine Learning

Artificial intelligence (AI) and machine learning are revolutionizing the field of social media marketing. These technologies enable marketers to analyze vast amounts of data, personalize content, and optimize campaigns with unprecedented precision. As AI continues to evolve, its impact on social media strategies grows, offering fresh insights and capabilities that were previously unimaginable.

Enhancing Data Analysis

One of the most significant advantages of AI and machine learning is their ability to process and analyze large datasets quickly and accurately. Traditional methods of data analysis can be time-consuming and prone to human error. In contrast, AI can sift through enormous amounts of data, identifying patterns and trends that might be missed by human analysts.

For instance, AI algorithms can analyze user behavior to predict future trends and preferences. This predictive analysis helps marketers anticipate what content will resonate with their audience, allowing for more strategic planning and content creation. By understanding these patterns, brands can tailor their messaging to meet the evolving needs and interests of their followers.

Personalizing User Experiences

Personalization is a cornerstone of effective social media marketing. AI-driven tools enable brands to deliver highly personalized experiences to their audience. Machine learning algorithms analyze individual user data, including past interactions, preferences, and behavior, to create customized content recommendations.

For example, AI can help determine the best time to post content for maximum engagement based on when specific users are most active. It can also suggest products or services tailored to an individual's interests, enhancing the relevance and appeal of marketing messages. This level of personalization not only improves user experience but also boosts engagement and conversion rates.

Automating Routine Tasks

AI-powered automation tools streamline many routine tasks involved in social media management. From scheduling posts to moderating comments, these tools free up valuable time for marketers to focus on strategic initiatives. Automation ensures consistency and efficiency, helping brands maintain a steady presence across various social media platforms.

Chatbots are a prime example of AI automation in action. These intelligent bots can handle customer inquiries in real-time, providing instant responses and solutions. By automating customer service, brands can offer 24/7 support, improving customer satisfaction and fostering stronger relationships.

Optimizing Ad Campaigns

AI and machine learning are transforming how brands approach social media advertising. AI algorithms analyze ad performance data to identify which elements drive the best results. This analysis covers various aspects, including audience targeting, ad placement, and creative elements.

For instance, AI can optimize ad spending by automatically adjusting bids based on real-time performance data. It can also A/B test different ad variations to determine which version resonates most with the target audience. These capabilities enable brands to maximize their return on investment and run more effective ad campaigns.

Enhancing Content Creation

Content creation is another area where AI and machine learning are making significant strides. AI-powered tools can generate content ideas, write social media posts, and even create visual assets. These tools analyze trending topics, user preferences, and engagement data to craft content that is likely to perform well.

For example, AI can help identify trending hashtags and keywords that can increase the visibility of posts. It can also suggest the best formats and styles for content based on audience preferences. By leveraging AI in content creation, brands can produce high-quality, engaging content more efficiently.

Monitoring and Sentiment Analysis

Understanding how your audience feels about your brand is crucial for effective social media marketing. AI-powered sentiment analysis tools scan social media platforms for mentions of your brand, analyzing the sentiment behind each mention. This analysis helps brands gauge public perception and respond appropriately.

For instance, if sentiment analysis reveals a surge in negative mentions, brands can quickly address the issues and take corrective actions. Conversely, positive sentiment can highlight successful strategies and areas to amplify. This real-time feedback loop enables brands to stay attuned to their audience's sentiments and adapt their strategies accordingly.

The Future of AI in Social Media Marketing

The integration of AI and machine learning in social media marketing is still in its early stages, with much more potential to be unlocked. As these technologies continue to advance, their applications will become even more sophisticated, offering deeper insights and more powerful tools for marketers.

Emerging trends such as augmented reality (AR), virtual reality (VR), and voice recognition are expected to further enhance the capabilities of AI in social media marketing. These innovations will provide new ways for brands to engage with their audience and deliver immersive, personalized experiences.

AI and machine learning are revolutionizing social media marketing by enhancing data analysis, personalizing user experiences, automating routine tasks, optimizing ad campaigns, aiding content creation, and providing real-time sentiment analysis. As these technologies continue to evolve, they will unlock even greater potential, enabling brands to connect with their audiences in more meaningful and impactful ways.

Evolving Consumer Behaviors

Digital transformation has fundamentally changed how consumers interact with brands. The rise of social media, mobile technology, and e-commerce platforms has created a more connected and informed consumer base. Today's consumers have unprecedented access to information and options, influencing their purchasing decisions and behaviors. Understanding these evolving behaviors is crucial for brands looking to stay relevant and competitive.

The Demand for Authenticity

Modern consumers value authenticity more than ever before. They seek genuine connections with brands that align with their values and beliefs. This shift has made transparency and honesty essential components of successful marketing strategies. Brands that demonstrate their commitment to ethical practices, social responsibility, and sustainability tend to resonate more with today's audience.

Consumers are also increasingly skeptical of traditional advertising. They prefer real, user-generated content and peer reviews over polished marketing messages. Influencer partnerships that feel genuine and unscripted often outperform highly produced campaigns. To engage effectively, brands must focus on building trust through authentic interactions and content.

The Rise of Social Commerce

Social media platforms have evolved from simple networking sites to powerful e-commerce channels. Features like shoppable posts, in-app purchases, and integrated payment systems have blurred the lines between social interaction and shopping. This evolution has given rise to social commerce, where consumers can discover, explore, and buy products directly within their favorite social media apps.

This seamless integration of shopping and social media offers convenience and immediacy, catering to consumers' desire for quick and easy transactions. Brands that leverage social commerce effectively can capitalize on impulse buying and enhance the overall shopping experience. This trend underscores the importance of a strong social media presence and strategic use of platform-specific features.

The Preference for Personalized Experiences

Personalization has become a key driver of consumer behavior. With the vast amount of data available, consumers expect brands to tailor their interactions and offerings to individual preferences. Personalized recommendations, targeted ads, and customized content create a more engaging and relevant user experience.

AI and machine learning play a significant role in delivering these personalized experiences. By analyzing user data, brands can anticipate needs, suggest products, and even predict future behavior. This level of personalization not only improves customer satisfaction but also fosters loyalty and increases conversion rates.

The Shift to Mobile First

The proliferation of smartphones has made mobile devices the primary tool for online activities, including shopping, social networking, and content consumption. As a result, mobile-first strategies are no longer optional but necessary for brands aiming to reach and engage their audience effectively.

Optimizing websites and content for mobile devices ensures a smooth and accessible user experience. Features like fast loading times, intuitive navigation, and mobile-friendly interfaces are critical. Additionally, mobile-specific platforms such as Instagram and TikTok offer unique opportunities to connect with consumers through visually engaging content.

The Influence of Reviews and Recommendations

Consumer decisions are heavily influenced by reviews and recommendations from peers and influencers. Online reviews, ratings, and testimonials provide social proof, helping potential customers make informed choices. Positive reviews can significantly boost a brand's credibility and attract new customers.

Brands should actively encourage satisfied customers to share their experiences online. Engaging with reviews—both positive and negative—demonstrates that a brand values customer feedback and is committed to improvement. Building a strong reputation through genuine customer reviews is an effective way to drive trust and loyalty.

The Growth of Subscription Services

Subscription services have gained popularity across various industries, offering convenience, cost savings, and personalized experiences. From streaming services and meal kits to beauty boxes and software subscriptions, this model caters to consumers' desire for curated, hassle-free options.

Brands adopting subscription models can benefit from predictable revenue streams and enhanced customer loyalty. Offering flexible subscription plans, personalized options, and exclusive perks can further entice consumers to commit to long-term relationships with the brand.

Adapting to Changing Consumer Preferences

Consumer preferences are dynamic, influenced by cultural trends, economic factors, and technological advancements. Brands must stay agile and responsive to these changes to remain competitive. Regularly conducting market research, analyzing consumer data, and staying attuned to industry trends are essential practices.

Engaging with your audience through social media, surveys, and feedback mechanisms can provide valuable insights into shifting preferences. Brands that listen to their customers and adapt their strategies accordingly can better meet their needs and expectations, ensuring sustained relevance and success.

Understanding and adapting to evolving consumer behaviors is crucial in today's fast-paced digital landscape. By focusing on authenticity, leveraging social commerce, personalizing experiences, prioritizing mobile, valuing reviews, embracing subscription models, and staying agile, brands can effectively navigate these changes and build strong, lasting connections with their audience.

Sustainable and Ethical Marketing

In today's market, consumers are increasingly prioritizing sustainability and ethical practices when choosing brands to support. Incorporating these values into your marketing strategy is not only good for the planet but also builds trust and loyalty among your audience. Here's how to effectively integrate sustainable and ethical practices into your marketing efforts.

Understanding Sustainability and Ethics

Sustainable and ethical marketing involves promoting products and practices that are environmentally friendly and socially responsible. This can include using eco-friendly materials, supporting fair labor practices, reducing carbon footprints, and engaging in charitable activities.

For example, a fashion brand committed to sustainability might use organic fabrics, implement fair trade practices, and promote recycling. These efforts should be communicated transparently to your audience to build credibility and trust.

Authentic Storytelling

Authenticity is crucial when it comes to sustainable and ethical marketing. Consumers are quick to spot greenwashing—when companies falsely claim to be environmentally friendly. Instead, focus on genuine efforts and communicate them transparently.

Share the story behind your sustainable practices. For instance, if your company has switched to renewable energy sources, explain the decision, the process, and the impact. Highlight real stories and data that illustrate your commitment to sustainability. This approach not only builds trust but also engages your audience emotionally.

Transparent Communication

Transparency is key to ethical marketing. Be open about your practices, both good and bad. If there are areas where you're still working to improve, share those goals and the steps you're taking to achieve them.

For instance, if your brand is aiming to reduce plastic use, communicate your current usage and your plans to switch to biodegradable materials. This honesty shows consumers that you are committed to continuous improvement and genuine about your efforts.

Engaging Your Audience

Involve your audience in your sustainability journey. Encourage them to participate and share their own sustainable practices. User-generated content showcasing customers using your eco-friendly products can be powerful testimonials.

For example, a skincare brand might invite customers to share their zero-waste beauty routines using the brand's products. This not only promotes your products but also fosters a community of like-minded individuals who value sustainability.

Collaborations and Partnerships

Partnering with other organizations that share your commitment to sustainability can amplify your impact. Collaborations can range from joint campaigns to product co-development with eco-friendly brands.

For instance, a beverage company might collaborate with a non-profit focused on clean water initiatives, donating a portion of profits to support their cause. Such partnerships enhance your credibility and extend your reach to new audiences who share similar values.

Measuring and Reporting Impact

Quantifying the impact of your sustainable practices is essential. Use metrics to track and report your progress. This could include reductions in carbon emissions, amounts of recycled materials used, or the number of fair trade suppliers you work with.

For example, a company might report that it has reduced its carbon footprint by 30% over the past year. Regularly sharing these metrics with your audience reinforces your commitment and demonstrates accountability.

Long-Term Commitment

Sustainable and ethical marketing is not a one-time campaign but a long-term commitment. It requires continuous effort and adaptation. Regularly update your practices and goals to reflect the evolving standards of sustainability.

For instance, as new eco-friendly technologies emerge, integrate them into your operations and communicate these advancements to your audience. This ongoing commitment ensures that your brand remains relevant and trusted.

Educating Your Audience

Part of sustainable marketing is educating your audience about the importance of environmental and social responsibility. Share informative content that highlights why sustainability matters and how they can contribute.

For example, a food brand might create content around the benefits of organic farming, both for health and the environment. This not only promotes your products but also raises awareness and encourages more sustainable choices among your audience.

Incorporating sustainable and ethical practices into your marketing strategy involves authentic storytelling, transparent communication, audience engagement, strategic collaborations, impact measurement, long-term commitment, and education. By genuinely embracing these principles, you can build a loyal and engaged customer base while making a positive impact on the world.

Conclusion

Navigating the ever-evolving landscape of social media marketing requires a blend of adaptability, authenticity, and strategic planning. Throughout this book, we have explored various strategies and tools to help you master social media marketing, from leveraging new platforms and creating compelling content to implementing sustainable and ethical practices.

In a world where digital interactions are pivotal in consumer decision-making, understanding the nuances of each platform and staying ahead of trends is essential. By embracing predictive analytics, automating workflows, and continuously reviewing and optimizing your strategies, you can ensure your marketing efforts are both efficient and impactful.

At the heart of social media marketing is engagement. Building meaningful connections with your audience through interactive content, authentic storytelling, and user-generated contributions fosters loyalty and drives long-term success. It's about more than just promoting products; it's about creating a community that shares your values and vision.

Sustainability and ethics are integral to a brand's identity and resonance with today's conscious consumers. Transparent communication and genuine efforts in these areas not only build trust but also differentiate your brand in a crowded marketplace.

As you move forward, remember that every success and failure offers valuable insights. Learning from these experiences allows you to refine your approach and continuously improve. Stay curious, stay adaptable, and stay committed to your goals.

The world of social media marketing is dynamic and filled with opportunities. By applying the strategies and insights shared in this book, you are well-equipped to navigate this landscape effectively, create meaningful connections, and drive unstoppable growth for your brand.

Dear Reader,

I hope you found this book insightful and valuable.

Your feedback is invaluable to me. If you enjoyed this book, I would appreciate it if you could take a moment to leave a review on the reading apps and platforms.

Thank you for your support, and I wish you all the best.

Kind regards,
Ghazwan

About the Author

Ghazwan is a passionate entrepreneur and business strategist dedicated to helping individuals and organizations achieve their full potential with a deep understanding of modern businesses' challenges and opportunities.

With a Master's degree in Computer and Systems Sciences from Stockholm University, specializing in eService design, requirement engineering, and business process management, he is equipped to innovate cutting-edge solutions.

He believes in the power of collaboration and lifelong learning, and his mission is to empower people to reach their goals and positively impact the world.

www.ingramcontent.com/pod-product-compliance
Lightning Source LLC
Chambersburg PA
CBHW052150220526
45471CB00004B/1605